CATHOLIC-JEWISH RELATIONS

Studies in Judaism and Christianity

Exploration of Issues in the Contemporary Dialogue between Christians and Jews

EDITORS

Michael McGarry, CSP
Adam Gregerman, PhD
Mark-David Janus, CSP, PhD
Yehezkel Landau, DMin
Peter Pettit, PhD
Elena Procario-Foley, PhD
Ellen M. Umansky, PhD
Rabbi Stephen Wylen

Catholic-Jewish Relations

Twelve Key Themes for Teaching & Preaching

Teresa Pirola

A STIMULUS BOOK

PAULIST PRESS • NEW YORK • MAHWAH, NJ

Unless otherwise indicated, the Scripture quotations contained herein are from the New Revised Standard Version: Catholic Edition, Copyright © 1989 and 1993, by the Division of Christian Education of the National Council of the Churches of Christ in the United States of America. Used by permission. All rights reserved.

Cover design by Joe Gallagher
Book design by Lynn Else

Copyright © 2023 by The Stimulus Foundation, Inc.

All rights reserved. No part of this publication may be reproduced, stored in a retrieval system, or transmitted in any form or by any means, electronic, mechanical, photocopying, recording, scanning, or otherwise, without either the prior written permission of the Publisher, or authorization through payment of the appropriate per-copy fee to the Copyright Clearance Center, Inc., 222 Rosewood Drive, Danvers, MA 01923, (978) 750-8400, fax (978) 646-8600, or on the Web at www.copyright.com. Requests to the Publisher for permission should be addressed to the Permissions Department, Paulist Press, 997 Macarthur Boulevard, Mahwah, NJ 07430.

Library of Congress Cataloging-in-Publication Data
Names: Pirola, Teresa, author.
Title: Catholic-Jewish relations : twelve key themes for teaching & preaching / Teresa Pirola.
Description: New York : Paulist Press, [2023] | Series: Studies in Judaism and Christianity | "A Stimulus book" —T.p. | Includes bibliographical references. | Summary: "This book is a guide to ground-breaking developments in modern Catholic-Jewish relations"—Provided by publisher.
Identifiers: LCCN 2022062195 (print) | LCCN 2022062196 (ebook) | ISBN 9780809156320 (paperback) | ISBN 9780809187942 (ebook)
Subjects: LCSH: Judaism—Relations—Catholic Church. | Catholic Church—Relations—Judaism.
Classification: LCC BM535 .P527 2023 (print) | LCC BM535 (ebook) | DDC 261.2/6—dc23/eng/20230414
LC record available at https://lccn.loc.gov/2022062195
LC ebook record available at https://lccn.loc.gov/2022062196

ISBN 978-0-8091-5632-0 (paperback)
ISBN 978-0-8091-8794-2 (e-book)

Published by Paulist Press
997 Macarthur Boulevard
Mahwah, New Jersey 07430
www.paulistpress.com

Printed and bound in the
United States of America

To the blessed memory of Jules & Laure Isaac

CONTENTS

Preface xi
Acknowledgments xvii
How to Use This Book xix
Abbreviations xxiii

TWELVE KEY THEMES 1

1. Jesus of Nazareth Was a Faithful Jew 3
   Key Points 3
   Notable Ecclesial Texts 4
   Exploring the Theme 6
   Checklist for Teachers and Homilists 13

2. The Church Can Never Forget Its
   Jewish Roots 15
   Key Points 15
   Notable Ecclesial Texts 16
   Exploring the Theme 18
   Checklist for Teachers and Homilists 23

3. God's Covenant with the Jewish People
   Is Alive and Active 25
   Key Points 25
   Notable Ecclesial Texts 26

CONTENTS

    Exploring the Theme 28
    Checklist for Teachers and Homilists...................... 35

4. The Old Testament Is Foundational to the
    New Testament.. 37
    Key Points.. 37
    Notable Ecclesial Texts... 38
    Exploring the Theme 41
    Checklist for Teachers and Homilists...................... 47

5. Christians and Jews Are United by Scripture,
    but also Divided 49
    Key Points.. 49
    Notable Ecclesial Texts... 50
    Exploring the Theme 53
    Checklist for Teachers and Homilists...................... 59

6. Judaism Is a Present-Day "Living Tradition"........... 61
    Key Points.. 61
    Notable Ecclesial Texts... 62
    Exploring the Theme 65
    Checklist for Teachers and Homilists...................... 73

7. Scripture Is to Be Interpreted without
    Anti-Jewish Bias 75
    Key Points.. 75
    Notable Ecclesial Texts... 76
    Exploring the Theme 79
    Checklist for Teachers and Homilists...................... 86

8. Antisemitism Is the Antithesis of the Gospel............. 88
    Key Points.. 88

Contents

    Notable Ecclesial Texts 89
    Exploring the Theme 93
    Checklist for Teachers and Homilists 100

9. Christians Learn Best about Judaism from Jews 102
    Key Points 102
    Notable Ecclesial Texts 103
    Exploring the Theme 105
    Checklist for Teachers and Homilists 111

10. Jews and Christians Work Together to Heal
       the World 113
    Key Points 113
    Notable Ecclesial Texts 114
    Exploring the Theme 116
    Checklist for Teachers and Homilists 122

11. The Catholic Church Does Not Seek to
       Convert Jews 123
    Key Points 123
    Notable Ecclesial Texts 124
    Exploring the Theme 127
    Checklist for Teachers and Homilists 136

12. The Land Is Integral to Jewish Experience 138
    Key Points 138
    Notable Ecclesial Texts 139
    Exploring the Theme 143
    Checklist for Teachers and Homilists 154

Afterword 156

CONTENTS

Appendix 1: Jules & Laure Isaac 159

Appendix 2: William Cooper 163

Glossary of Terms 167

Notes 171

List of Works Cited 185

PREFACE

Within the last six decades an extraordinary development has been unfolding in the Catholic Church. At various levels of magisterial authority—beginning with its most solemn expression, an ecumenical council—popes and bishops and theologians have been speaking about Jews and Judaism in a way that is new and innovative, and yet, in another sense, as old and continuous as the most ancient roots of the church itself.

This delicate dance of novelty and conservatism signals a movement of authentic reform. Faithful to the teachings of the Second Vatican Council (1962–65) and attentive to the theological renewal movement of *ressourcement* ("return to the sources"), the postconciliar task has been to free Christian expression from its toxic anti-Jewish distortions of the past, while holding fast to those precious threads of biblical and credal continuity by which the church lives "in contact with its deepest tradition."[1] In contrast to what occurred in previous centuries, no longer is it the commonplace Christian response to treat Jews with reservation and suspicion, much less to regard them as "enemies" of the church. Now the vocabulary of official Catholic documents draws on words like "respect," "reconciliation," "mutual enrichment" and "dialogue" to describe the proper attitude of Christians toward their Jewish brothers and sisters.

This new language has not flowed easily. There was fierce debate, even opposition, within and outside the Second Vatican Council as the council fathers grappled with the complexities at hand—pragmatic and political as well as theological and pastoral. Eventually, reaching deeply into biblical memory, including a notable Pauline text, there emerged statements of vital importance about how Catholics viewed their relationship with the Jewish people. These statements honored the Jewish identity of Jesus and the Jewish roots of Christianity; they affirmed God's steadfast love for and fidelity to the Jewish people; they unmasked the evil of anti-Jewish tropes, repudiated every form of antisemitism, and called for "fraternal dialogue" between Christians and Jews.

These points were succinctly expressed in the conciliar Declaration on the Relationship of the Church to Non-Christian Religions, *Nostra Aetate* (Latin: "In our time"). A short document, which also addresses the wider landscape of interreligious dialogue, *Nostra Aetate* effectively reset the Catholic magisterial compass with respect to Judaism and was to prove influential for other churches as well. Importantly, its theological core found expression in two other conciliar documents, both dogmatic constitutions and therefore teachings bearing the highest authoritative weight: *Lumen Gentium* and *Verbum Dei*, on "the church" and on "divine revelation," respectively. By the time *Nostra Aetate* came to be promulgated on October 28, 1965, a new era in Catholic-Jewish relations was underway.

As Catholic-Jewish dialogue proceeded in the years and decades following the council, it built upon the prophetic, fledgling efforts of small groups of Christian and Jewish scholars and animators who had been engaging in study and dialogue since the 1920s.[2] Meanwhile, other Christian churches were producing similar documents of their own with the intention of repudiating antisemitism and expressing a positive stance toward Judaism. Nor did the change stop there. As the dialogue uncovered layer

Preface

upon layer of harm done to the Jewish people, it called Christians to an ever-deepening examination of conscience and a reappraisal of the way they understood and communicated their own cherished beliefs. Christians were coming to appreciate that at its roots Christianity is so entwined with Judaism that it is impossible to reflect on Jesus Christ and the gospel without also reflecting on God's presence and activity in and among the Jewish people. What began at Vatican II as a corrective of a wrong was fast becoming an opportunity to ponder afresh the mystery of the church itself, vis-a-vis God's faithful love for and election of Israel.[3] The more Christians grew in appreciation of the vitality of the covenantal life by which Jews lived in relationship with God, the more they were confronted with questions about how present-day Christianity should relate to present-day Judaism. Indeed, some of these paths of reflection led to questions of such immense theological depths that no definitive answers were forthcoming; the questions could only be held patiently, respectfully, within a framework of continuing interreligious conversation, study, and friendship.

Six decades after Vatican II, much has been achieved. In specialist circles and at high levels of interfaith dialogue—among academics and ecclesial leaders—Christians, with Jewish interlocutors, are exploring new questions in lively, fruitful exchanges; these include the significance of the Jewishness of Jesus and the Jewish roots of Christianity, the value of Jewish Torah interpretation to Christian biblical studies, covenantal understandings, the nuances of "mission," and the Jewish bond with the holy land. In this way, the Jewish-Christian relationship is being taken forward, new ground is being broken. Formulations that came into use in the Catholic Church under the influence of Pope John Paul II's papacy—notably, the conviction that God's covenant with the Jewish people is "never revoked"—are

CATHOLIC-JEWISH RELATIONS

gaining traction and entering mainstream Catholic teaching. At the same time, in some scholarly circles there are voices expressing reservation about the new momentum, fearing that it may be moving too fast and too far, built upon assumptions that are not fully tested and that require further study. Their voices add value to the dialogue and deserve a considered response. Some cautionary voices are concerned that an emphasis on innovation comes at the expense of an appreciation of *Nostra Aetate*'s continuity with the tradition; that in the enthusiasm to embrace positive relations with Jews there remain uncomfortable questions that go unanswered; that certain statements in the dialogue widely accepted as the teaching of the Catholic Church are in fact not "settled" doctrine. Some even go as far as to question the doctrinal authority of *Nostra Aetate* itself, claiming that its status does not go beyond "pastoral illustration" of *Lumen Gentium*, a position robustly rebutted by other Vatican II scholars.

Meanwhile, outside these specialist circles, a very different situation exists at the "coal face" of church life. Generally speaking, in this author's Australian Catholic context at least, the conversation about Jewish-Christian relations is notable for its rarity. While certain excellent fruits of the dialogue are taken for granted (revised textbooks in high schools, for example), actual widespread knowledge of developments in the Jewish-Christian dialogue is generally lacking in the pews as well as the pulpits. Many Catholics today know little or nothing about the far-reaching impact of *Nostra Aetate* let alone about the dialogue conducted by Vatican officials and Catholic scholars with their Jewish counterparts. Catholics are generally aware that their church concerns itself with a wide range of issues such as prayer, liturgy, sacraments, family, youth, the role of women, sexuality, bioethics, evangelization, ecology, indigenous

Preface

reconciliation, refugees, poverty, human trafficking. They may even be aware that the church is interested in "interreligious" matters addressing peace and societal cohesion. But that the church is undertaking a game-changing journey in its relationship with the Jewish people; that this shift in relationship is impacting the church's own self-understanding; and that this journey is necessary in view of the conditioning effects of centuries of Christian anti-Judaism are not well known and rarely heard from pulpits or in classrooms. The faithful may have seen the footage of Pope John Paul II praying at the Western Wall in Jerusalem in 2000, but the significance of the event escapes them. They still hear sermons with anti-Jewish bias. Many have never met a Jew. Pernicious stereotypes are all too easily accessed online. Even the term *antisemitism* is becoming less, not better, understood, reflecting problems in society at large. The fruits of Vatican II are undeniable, but the trickle-down reception of these breakthroughs is slow, with steps taken both forward and backward.

Here we come to the purpose of this book. It offers a brief road map for busy people—teachers, parents, clergy, religious, laity—to become acquainted with the main themes and documents of the Catholic-Jewish dialogue, distilled here as twelve key statements.[4] Framed by the author's Roman Catholic tradition, and written for a Catholic audience, it is the "quick read" path to upskilling in this area, while providing leads for further reading and discussion. My intention in its writing is that the gains of the past sixty years become better known to nonspecialists and grassroots audiences, especially those engaged in teaching, preaching, and shaping the minds and hearts of the next generation.

Only a little can be said in a short publication, however I trust it will be enough to instill a wakeful, informed

CATHOLIC-JEWISH RELATIONS

curiosity about what is arguably the most exciting and far-reaching development in the Catholic Church today: a reawakening to the Jewish foundations of Christian faith and the church's ongoing path of reconciliation and partnership with the Jewish people.

ACKNOWLEDGMENTS

My personal journey into the world of Jewish-Christian relations has been a "slow burn" over decades. It began with my first interfaith experiences as a child growing up with Jewish neighbors and classmates in New Rochelle, New York, in the 1970s. Other seeds were sown along the way. However, it wasn't until much later, 2007, following a graced invitation to come to Bat Kol Institute Jerusalem (where Jewish teachers guided Christian students in Torah study), that the penny really dropped as to the extraordinary significance of *Nostra Aetate* and the resulting path taken by the Catholic Church. From there, the learning curve began in earnest, and my Light of Torah ministry emerged.

Given the number of people who have been part of this journey and therefore who have, directly or indirectly, contributed to the birthing of this book, forgive me for taking the safe route of a universal "thank you." When I look back on these pages, I am grateful to all who have generously provided feedback, critique, and encouragement at various stages of manuscript drafts. I acknowledge those who have shaped and challenged my thinking through their writings, teachings, music, prayer, hospitality, and table talk, sometimes as hosts or traveling companions in the Holy Land; and those who, at crucial junctures, offered practical support to enable the "next step." I am grateful to Jewish friends who have opened my Catholic eyes to the wide spectrum of Jewish life; Christian friends who have provided fertile ground for exploring ways to engage grassroots audiences with the vision of *Nostra Aetate*; and gracious Muslim friends who have also been part of this journey. I am indebted to colleagues with whom I have collaborated in interfaith education initiatives; to teachers and supervisors who have guided my studies; and I am forever in awe of the scholars, past and present, working in this space of Jewish-Christian relations.

Most especially, I am deeply grateful to the Stimulus Foundation and the team at Paulist Press for enabling this work to be published. And, to momentarily rescind the decision not to use names, I thank Vince Casey for his all-weather steadfast friendship in life and ministry; and my family, especially my parents, Ron and Mavis, for their ever-generous love and support. And the late Jack Driscoll, CFC, dear friend and mentor. He would have been delighted to see this book published.

HOW TO USE THIS BOOK

This book is designed as an educational guide for teachers and clergy and other formators in the Catholic faith. A "quick" read will bring the reader up to date with key issues of the Catholic-Jewish dialogue. A "slow" read will take the reader on a journey through the documents of the Catholic Church pertaining to Jewish-Christian relations since the Second Vatican Council.

The book is structured to assist teaching forums for general audiences. Each of twelve chapters presents a key insight reflected in the emerging direction of the official Catholic-Jewish dialogue conducted by the Vatican.

> Each chapter opens with a few salient points for quick reference.
> This is followed by a selection of quotations, predominantly drawn from official ecclesial documents of the Roman Catholic Church. They are of varying authoritative weights and many of them are influential and frequently quoted in circles of Jewish-Christian dialogue. This section allows the reader to hear directly what the Catholic Church is "saying" about its relationship with the Jewish people, through a range of voices from various forums of engagement.
> Next, there is a brief discussion of the chapter theme.

CATHOLIC-JEWISH RELATIONS

Finally, a series of pointed questions invites readers to assess their own grasp of the issues at hand: In what way is my teaching or preaching in tune with Catholic teaching regarding the presentation of Jews and Judaism in catechesis; and in what way is my practice being challenged to develop and change?

A list of cited works provides a starting point for further study of the key themes.

THE LIMITS OF THIS BOOK

Being a short introductory work on Catholic-Jewish relations, there are certain topics that lie beyond the parameters of this book. It does not, for example, explore how Jews and Christians relate to Islam. The trilateral dialogue of the three "Abrahamic" religions is of vital importance;[1] however it is beyond the scope of this discussion.

Nor does this book explore the range of post-Holocaust responses to Judaism emanating from across the Christian world, beyond the Catholic Church. Having said that, much of what is written here finds common ground with other mainstream Christian churches undertaking a similar passage in reflection, dialogue, and reconciliation with the Jewish people. Indeed, the ecumenical implications of this journey are immense.

In discussing Judaism, too, there are inherent limits. In what follows, frequent references to "the Jewish people" often presume certain spiritual and covenantal perspectives that, while generally accepted by observant adherents to Judaism, are not shared by all Jews, or are understood with varying nuances according to the range of denominational expressions of Judaism. While the Catholic Church

How to Use This Book

approaches Judaism as one religious tradition approaching another, there are many self-identifying Jews who do not define themselves in religious terms.

Further, the church lens employed by this book views Judaism as having profound significance for Christianity—a view not reciprocated by Jews engaging with Christianity. As is often pointed out in circles of dialogue, Christians "need" Judaism in order to be Christian in a way that Jews do not "need" Christianity in order to be Jews. Thus, the question sometimes arises: Does the asymmetry of approach lead to a certain (unintended) "appropriation" of Judaism for Christian purposes? The question is complicated further by sensitivities arising from our fraught history. For some Jews, any Christian attempt to theologize about Judaism will understandably be suspect: Is this yet another attempt by Christians to define, control, and dominate Jewish lives?

Stepping into this minefield of sensitivities, this book traverses only a small part of a complex terrain. I acknowledge, and I ask the reader to remain cognizant throughout, that the Church is still in the very beginning stages of rediscovering its relationship with the Jewish people, and that this path, with all its nuances and complexities, must be trod "lightly," respectfully, humbly, allowing breathing room for "more" to occur, for further insights to unfold in due course. On the one hand, fidelity to scripture and tradition requires Catholics to step forward boldly into this new theological and pastoral space opened by Vatican II and to enter into robust, life-giving discussions on a range of issues. On the other hand, no attempt at progress can or should be "forced" onto the Jewish-Christian relationship, as this would be detrimental to that very relationship. From the standpoint of faith, we swim in an ocean of divine mystery over which no one but the author of that mystery has ultimate control. At the end of the day, a believer can only trust that all things find their place and meaning and proper timing in the fullness of truth and love. This book is offered in that spirit.

Sources

Unless they appear as part of a quoted ecclesial text, scripture quotations are from the New Revised Standard Version Bible.

Unless otherwise indicated, excerpts from official ecclesial documents and other writings of significance for the Catholic-Jewish dialogue have been sourced from the *Dialogika* online library maintained by the Council of Centers on Jewish-Christian Relations and the Institute for Jewish-Catholic Relations of Saint Joseph's University, Philadelphia, https://www.ccjr.us/dialogika-resources/documents-and-statements/roman-catholic.

The "Checklist" sections in this book are based on an adaptation of criteria listed in "Methods and Criteria for Assessing Texts," chapter 5 in Philip Cunningham, *Education for Shalom: Religion Textbooks and the Enhancement of the Catholic and Jewish Relationship* (Collegeville, MN: Liturgical Press, 1995).

ABBREVIATIONS

CCC	*Catechism of the Catholic Church*
CRRJ	Pontifical Commission for Religious Relations with the Jews
DV	*Dei Verbum*, Dogmatic Constitution on Divine Revelation, Second Vatican Council, November 18, 1965
EG	*Evangelii Gaudium*, The Joy of the Gospel, Apostolic Exhortation on the Proclamation of the Gospel in Today's World, Pope Francis, November 24, 2013
"Gifts and Calling"	"'The Gifts and the Calling of God Are Irrevocable' (Rom 11:29). A Reflection on Theological Questions Pertaining to Catholic-Jewish Relations on the Occasion of the 50th Anniversary of 'Nostra Aetate' (No. 4),″ Commission for Religious Relations With the Jews, December 10, 2015
"Guidelines"	"Guidelines and Suggestions for Implementing the Conciliar Declaration 'Nostra Aetate' (No. 4),″ Commission for Religious Relations With the Jews, December 1, 1974
ICCJ	International Council of Christians & Jews
IHRA	International Holocaust Remembrance Alliance
LG	*Lumen Gentium*, Dogmatic Constitution on the Church, Second Vatican Council, November 21, 1964
NA	*Nostra Aetate*, Declaration on the Relationship of the Church to Non-Christian Religions, Second Vatican Council, October 28, 1965
NCCB	National Conference of Catholic Bishops (USA)

CATHOLIC-JEWISH RELATIONS

"Notes"	"Notes on the Correct Way to Present the Jews and Judaism in Preaching and Catechesis in the Roman Catholic Church," Commission for Religious Relations With the Jews, June 24, 1985
NRSV	New Revised Standard Version
PBC	Pontifical Biblical Commission
SCJR	*Studies in Christian-Jewish Relations*
Vatican II	Second Vatican Council
VD	*Verbum Domini*, Post-Synodal Apostolic Exhortation on the Word of God in the Life and Mission of the Church, Pope Benedict XVI, September 30, 2010

TWELVE KEY THEMES

...the Jews and Judaism should not occupy an occasional and marginal place in catechesis: their presence there is essential and should be organically integrated.

CRRJ, "Notes," I.2

1

JESUS OF NAZARETH WAS A FAITHFUL JEW

KEY POINTS

This chapter begins with a plain historical fact: *Jesus was a Jew*. As we shall see, this has profound theological implications.

- Jesus, Mary, the apostles, and most of Jesus' earliest disciples were Jews. They understood themselves to be descendants of Abraham, Isaac, and Jacob, and heirs to the teachings, promises, and covenants of God.
- The Catholic Church acknowledges Jesus' Jewish identity as a fact of history. Further, this history is seen to have weighty biblical, theological, and spiritual meaning for Christians.
- To acknowledge Jesus as a Jew includes affirming his ancestral story recounted in the Hebrew Scriptures/Old Testament.
- The Jewishness of Jesus is integral to the Christian doctrine of the incarnation, the belief that "the Word became flesh and lived among us" (John 1:14). In Jesus, God didn't become "human" in the abstract; God became a Jew.

TWELVE KEY THEMES

"Whoever meets Jesus Christ, meets Judaism" (Pope John Paul II, Mainz, 1980).

NOTABLE ECCLESIAL TEXTS

Second Vatican Council

There is, first, that people to whom the covenants and promises were made, and from whom Christ was born according to the flesh (cf. Rom 9:4–5).

LG 16

The Church keeps ever in mind the words of the Apostle about his kinsmen: "theirs is the sonship and the glory and the covenants and the law and the worship and the promises; theirs are the fathers and from them is the Christ according to the flesh" (Rom 9:4–5), the Son of the Virgin Mary. She also recalls that the Apostles, the Church's main-stay and pillars, as well as most of the early disciples who proclaimed Christ's Gospel to the world, sprang from the Jewish people.

NA 4

Pontifical Commission for Religious Relations with the Jews

Jesus was and always remained a Jew, his ministry was deliberately limited "to the lost sheep of the house of Israel" (Matt 15:24). Jesus is fully a man of his time, and of his environment—the Jewish Palestinian one of the first century, the anxieties and hopes of which he shared. This cannot but underline both the reality of the Incarnation and the very meaning of the history of salvation, as it has been revealed in the Bible (Rom 1:3–4; Gal 4:4–5).

"Notes," III.12

Pope John Paul II

Jesus' human identity is determined on the basis of his bond with the people of Israel, with the dynasty of David and his descent from Abraham. And this does not mean only a physical belonging. By taking part in the synagogue celebrations where the Old Testament texts were read and commented on, Jesus also came humanly to know these texts; he nourished his mind and heart with them, using them in prayer and as an inspiration for his actions....

To deprive Christ of his relationship with the Old Testament is, therefore, to detach him from his roots and to empty his mystery of all meaning. Indeed, to be meaningful, the Incarnation had to be rooted in centuries of preparation. Christ would otherwise have been like a meteor that falls to the earth and is devoid of any connection with human history.

From her origins, the Church has well understood that the Incarnation is rooted in history and, consequently, she has fully accepted Christ's insertion into the history of the People of Israel.

Address to the Pontifical Biblical Commission,
April 11, 1997, 3–4

TWELVE KEY THEMES

Pope Benedict XVI

Jesus, a son of the Chosen People, was born, lived and died a Jew (cf. Rom 9:4–5). Mary, his Mother, likewise invites us to rediscover the Jewish roots of Christianity. These close bonds are a unique treasure of which Christians are proud and for which they are indebted to the Chosen People.

Post-Synodal Apostolic Exhortation on the Church in the Middle East, Ecclesia in Medio Oriente, September 14, 2012, 20

Pontifical Commission for Religious Relations with the Jews

One cannot understand Jesus' teaching or that of his disciples without situating it within the Jewish horizon in the context of the living tradition of Israel; one would understand his teachings even less so if they were seen in opposition to this tradition.

...Fully and completely human, a Jew of his time, descendant of Abraham, son of David, shaped by the whole tradition of Israel, heir of the prophets, Jesus stands in continuity with his people and its history.

"Gifts and Calling," 14

EXPLORING THE THEME

Jesus was a Jew. Not a Christian. Not an apostate Jew. He was a faithful Jew who lived and worked in the first century of the Common Era, largely in the region of Galilee. Historical scholarship, biblical testimony, and Catho-

Jesus of Nazareth Was a Faithful Jew

lic teaching all converge in agreement on this point about Jesus' Jewish identity: he was born of a Jewish woman and circumcised on the eighth day; he identified with the ancestral traditions of Israel and lived his life within the parameters of the Judaism of his time. He frequented the temple and the synagogue, observed Jewish purity laws, kept the Sabbath, and celebrated Jewish festivals according to the customs of his day. He prayed Jewish prayers, taught from the Torah, and entered into robust discussions about its interpretation. Whatever disagreements Jesus had with other Jews, as depicted in the Gospels, these are understood to be intra-Jewish debates typical of the religious and cultural dynamics of his day.

The fact and importance of Jesus' Jewish identity was a key teaching of the Second Vatican Council (*LG* 16; *NA* 4). There, Jewish identity is affirmed not only for Jesus, but also for Mary, the apostles, and most of the early disciples. Why did the council deem it necessary to focus on the historical fact of Jesus' Jewish identity, and why should we continue to consider it today? After all, isn't the Jewishness of Jesus an obvious, albeit incidental, fact of history that Christians can presume and then "move on" to more important spiritual matters?

In order to appreciate both the question and its answer, it is necessary to contextualize the Second Vatican Council and to recall the long history of Christian ambiguity toward Jesus' Jewish identity whereby Christian culture (as distinct from defined doctrine) routinely downplayed or ignored Jesus' Jewishness. In the mind of many Christians, Jesus of Nazareth was not really a Jew but a Christian. Such distorted views of history fed into dark forces that culminated in the pro-Aryan racial theories of the twentieth century and bolstered Hitler's genocidal agenda. From this starting point we can immediately appreciate

TWELVE KEY THEMES

the necessity and healing influence of the council's teaching and the challenge it posed to Catholics in the 1960s. Consider, for example, that just a few decades prior to the council, a certain prominent Catholic religious order still had in place a 350-year-old ban on the admission of anyone with Jewish ancestry. It was deemed acceptable for a well-regarded, Rome-based Catholic periodical to publish material infected by anti-Jewish polemic. In Europe of the 1930s, a number of high-profile Catholic intellectuals featured among those who promoted antisemitic, pro-Aryan racial theories. In one case, a particularly influential and popular Catholic preacher in Austria publicly proposed the idea that Jews were genetically defective due to being mired in a special kind of sinfulness that defied even the saving power of the sacrament of baptism.[1] Especially alarming is the willingness to tolerate such thinking among much of the population of a Europe that had been "Christianized" for centuries. It would seem that, for many Christians, the Jewishness of their own savior, and the Jewishness of Mary and the apostles, had little influence on their attitudes toward Jews generally.

Contrast this situation with the teaching of the Second Vatican Council (1962–65). Just twenty years after the Second World War had ended, with comprehension of the diabolical reality of the Holocaust taking effect in Christian consciences, Catholic bishops from around the world gathered in their highest-ranking assembly to formulate authoritative teachings for the renewal of the Catholic Church. Not only did they publicly acknowledge and affirm the fact of Jesus' Jewishness, they recognized Jewish ancestral lineage ("Abraham's stock," *NA* 4) to be integral to the spiritual bedrock of the mystery of the church.

This teaching marked a radical shift for the Catholic Church. In taking this step, the council fathers were seek-

Jesus of Nazareth Was a Faithful Jew

ing to correct a terrible wrong: the long history of Christian antagonism toward Jews that French historian Jules Isaac famously labeled "the teaching of contempt."[2] The "teaching of contempt," of course, was never doctrinally articulated as part of the church's deposit of faith. However, the phrase captures an attitude, a sentiment, an ideological slant that for centuries had infected catechetics, homiletics, theological writings, and even aspects of the liturgy. Facing into centuries of this aberration in Christian thought, the council repudiated the centuries-old accusation that the Jews were collectively responsible for the death of Jesus. It denounced antisemitism and charted the beginnings of a fresh path—a way of thinking about and relating to Jews and Judaism that signaled the recovery of an authentic continuity with deep defining truths of Christianity.

It is fitting to pause and ponder this radical shift and ask ourselves how it impacts our thinking and teaching today. To return to our earlier question: Why was it important for the Catholic Church of the 1960s to come to grips with Jesus' Jewishness? And why is it important for us today? This is a searching question to pose to a congregation or a class of students, or to stimulate conversation and thinking in family or friendship circles. Presumably, a first response will be to declare the injustice of treating *any* human being with prejudice and contempt. Clearly, the affirmation of Jesus' Jewishness touches the central nerve of antisemitic discourse. Antisemitism, like all forms of racism and bigotry, is a sin against human dignity. It has no place in any just and compassionate society, let alone in Christian communities that preach the gospel. The universal value of respect for human dignity grounds the council's affirmation of Jesus' Jewishness.

But is it the only reason operative here? In fact, the teaching of Vatican II draws also from another well of insight; one with pointed relevance to the unique claims of Christian faith itself. Let us unpack this assertion by way of four statements:

1. "Thus he became an authentic son of Israel"[3]

To recognize Jesus as a Jew is to engage the story of salvation in its entirety. When Christians proclaim that "the Word became flesh" (John 1:14), they are acknowledging that Jesus didn't appear out of the blue "like a meteor that falls to the earth and is devoid of any connection with human history."[4] Rather, his appearance on the stage of history has a formidable "backstory"—the long history of God's faithful presence and action in the community of Israel. To remember Jesus as Jew is to remember not only the limited years of his earthly life, but the whole story of salvation. In other words, the "Jesus story" doesn't simply begin with the New Testament. The Jesus of the Gospels is inextricable from the religious memory of the people of Israel, a memory recounted in the Jewish Scriptures that the church has inherited and canonically integrated into its Old Testament. Staying connected to both Old and New Testaments, to the "big picture" of salvation history, is indispensable for authentic Christian faith.

2. "Born of a woman, born under the law" (Gal 4:4)

In St. Paul's Letter to the Galatians, we find Jesus' Jewish identity expressed in this succinct christological formula: "But when the fullness of time had come, God sent his Son, born of a woman, born under the law" (Gal 4:4); that is, born of a *Jewish* woman, born *as a Jew*. What can we learn from this? How beautifully relational are the designs of God! The story of salvation is inseparable from family, peoplehood, community, the collective experience. In short, redemption is lived in relational terms with a relational God. This is true of the Savior himself, who as the God-man enters human history as the fruit of Jewish covenantal life, his identity firmly planted in the ancestral memory of Abraham and Sarah, Isaac and Rebekah, Jacob and Rachel and Leah. In the Gospels Jesus is recognized in relational terms: he is identified as a son of Israel, a son of David, the son of a Jewish woman, Son of God. To know the person of Jesus is to know him as "familied." An isolated, "lone ranger" Jesus standing apart from his Jewish people is not the Jesus of history, is not the Christ of the Gospels. Jewish identity is perennially relevant to the Jesus encountered in history and through faith.

3. "...and from them is the Christ according to the flesh"[5]

Christian tradition readily speaks of God becoming "man," that is, "human." Whilst this is true, no human being exists as a generic "human." In Jesus of Nazareth the revelation of God could only occur through the concrete and the particular, and not manifested through an abstract "genre" that we call "humanity" or "flesh."[6] The startling claim of Christianity that the Word of God became incarnate refers, in the first place, not to a universal symbol, idea, metaphor, value, ethic, or philosophy, but to an embodied personal life.

The doctrine of the incarnation, then, effectively proclaims, not that God become an abstraction, but that *God became a Jew*. And to be a Jew is to belong to the Jewish people. It is in and through *this* people, *this* covenant, *this* mother, and *this* miracle child that the mystery of God's word takes flesh. We may wish to pause at this point and take a breath to process this claim. It can be quite confronting if we are not accustomed to viewing the incarnation through such a lens. Yet it is an insight found embedded in the thirteenth-century writings of St. Thomas Aquinas who insisted that Jesus had to be born of a Jewish mother in order to be the true messiah, Son of God.[7] Jewish ancestry, life, and relationships are integral to the very core of Christian faith.

4. "Whoever meets Jesus Christ, meets Judaism"[8]

In one short sentence Pope John Paul II states the enduring relevance of Jesus' earthly Jewish existence for Christians. Note that the sentence does not read, "Whoever met Jesus in first-century Galilee met a Jew." That is true and a given. Here, his statement suggests that what was true in the first century continues to resonate as a perennial, present-day meeting point. A Christian who encounters the risen Jesus today—through the scriptures, through prayer, through the community of faith—encounters Judaism. Jesus' Jewish identity is not a label he can take off and lay aside, even as the risen and glorified One. Such is Christian belief in bodily resurrection. Jesus' earthly story (the relational story we encounter in the Gospels) continues to inform his personal identity in resurrection and glory. *Whoever meets Jesus Christ, meets Judaism.*

The plain fact of Jesus' Jewishness, then, is a non-negotiable element of reflection for authentic Christian faith. There may be something in our Christian sensibilities that recoils at this assertion. It can sound too specific, too raw, too "earthly," too *limited*. After all, isn't Jesus Christ the Second Person of the Blessed Trinity, Lord of the universe, Savior of the world? All this is clearly affirmed by Christian belief. Christ is truly God *and* truly man, with an earthly story as a first-century Jew that we continue to remember and encounter through Sacred Scripture. What is transcendent and universal is made known by way of the particular, concrete, historical event. Unless Christian faith remains anchored to the reality of Jesus' earthly identity, it flirts with Gnosticism. It risks being reduced to a religion of inner spiritual sentiment, intellectual elitism, or psychological well-being, when in fact the radical innovation of the gospel is the proclamation that the savior of the world comes "according to the flesh" (Rom 9:5).

Christian commentators often speak of the "scandal" of the incarnation. In Jesus' Jewishness, Christians are confronted by the gospel proclamation of the "enfleshed" God. The teaching of Vatican II calls the faithful to embrace the "scandal" of the Jewish Jesus.

CHECKLIST FOR TEACHERS AND HOMILISTS

Is the Jewish identity of Jesus, Mary, the apostles, and the early disciples of Jesus clear in my teachings or homilies? Or are they depicted as "Christians" rather than as Jews?

When employing visual images of Jesus, Mary, and the apostles in the classroom, are they ever depicted as identifiably Jewish (e.g., wearing a prayer shawl, holding a Torah scroll)? Or is their appearance always anything but Jewish?

Does my teaching or preaching communicate reverence for the Old Testament and the ancestral story that envelops the Jesus we meet in the Gospels? Or do I leave my listeners with the impression that the Old Testament and the long history of the people of Israel have little

TWELVE KEY THEMES

or nothing to do with the life and ministry of Jesus?

Is Jesus' earthly story as a faithful, Torah-observant Jew evident in my teaching or preaching? Or is my audience left only with the impression of a Jesus opposed to Jewish norms, or of a Jesus who stood outside his Jewish tradition?

2

THE CHURCH CAN NEVER FORGET ITS JEWISH ROOTS

KEY POINTS

This chapter continues to explore Jesus' Jewish identity in relation to the beginnings of Christianity.

- Given the Jewish identity of Jesus, Mary, the apostles, and Jesus' early disciples, the foundations of Christianity are anchored in Jewish covenantal life.
- This history has shaped, and continues to influence, the church's self-understanding today—biblically, theologically, liturgically, spiritually.
- The church discovers its permanent link with Judaism by pondering the depths of its own mystery.[1]
- The olive tree is an apt biblical image for describing the reconciled relationship between Jews and Gentiles (Rom 11:17–24), and between Israel and the church (NA 4).

TWELVE KEY THEMES

NOTABLE ECCLESIAL TEXTS

Pope Pius XI

Through Christ and in Christ we are the spiritual descendants of Abraham....Spiritually, we are Semites.

Reflection given to Belgian pilgrims,
September 6, 1938

Second Vatican Council

As the sacred synod searches into the mystery of the Church, it remembers the bond that spiritually ties the people of the New Covenant to Abraham's stock....

Nor can [the Church] forget that she draws sustenance from the root of that well-cultivated olive tree onto which have been grafted the wild shoots, the Gentiles (cf. Rom 11:17–24).

NA 4

Pontifical Commission for Religious Relations with the Jews

Abraham is truly the father of our faith (Rom 4:11–12; Roman Canon: *patriarchae nostri Abrahae*). And it is said (1 Cor 10:1): "Our fathers were all under the cloud, and all passed through the sea." The patriarchs, prophets, and other personalities of the Old Testament have been venerated and always will be venerated as saints in the liturgical tradition of the Oriental Church as also of the Latin Church....

The Church Can Never Forget Its Jewish Roots

All this should help us to understand better what St. Paul says (Rom 11:16ff) about the "root" and the "branches." The Church and Christianity, for all their novelty, find their origin in the Jewish milieu of the first century of our era, and more deeply still in the "design of God" (*NA*, 4), realized in the Patriarchs, Moses, and the Prophets, down to its consummation in Christ Jesus.

"Notes," II.2, III.9

Pope John Paul II

The Church of Christ discovers her "bond" with Judaism by "searching into her own mystery" (cf. *NA*, 4). The Jewish religion is not "extrinsic" to us, but in a certain way is "intrinsic" to our own religion. With Judaism therefore we have a relationship which we do not have with any other religion. You are our dearly beloved brothers and, in a certain way, it could be said that you are our elder brothers.

Address at the Great Synagogue of Rome, April 13, 1986

Pontifical Commission for Religious Relations with the Jews

For Jewish-Christian dialogue in the first instance God's covenant with Abraham proves to be constitutive, as he is not only the father of Israel but also the father of the faith of Christians....This recourse to the Abrahamic covenant is so essentially constitutive of the Christian faith that the

TWELVE KEY THEMES

Church without Israel would be in danger of losing its locus in the history of salvation.

"Gifts and Calling," 33

Pope Benedict XVI

Saint Paul also uses the lovely image of the olive tree to describe the very close relationship between Christians and Jews: the Church of the Gentiles is like a wild olive shoot, grafted onto the good olive tree that is the people of the Covenant (cf. Rom 11:17–24). In other words, we draw our nourishment from the same spiritual roots.

VD 43

Pope Francis

From a theological point of view, it is clear there is an inseparable bond between Christians and Jews. Christians, to be able to understand themselves, cannot not refer to their Jewish roots, and the Church, while professing salvation through faith in Christ, recognizes the irrevocability of the Covenant and God's constant and faithful love for Israel.

Address at the Great Synagogue of Rome,
January 17, 2016

EXPLORING THE THEME

Where does Christianity begin? Here, let us take as our starting point its roots in Jewish life of the first century of the Common Era.

With the destruction of the Jewish Temple in 70 CE,

The Church Can Never Forget Its Jewish Roots

Jewish communities suffered a catastrophic blow. At the hands of the Romans, the uprising in Jerusalem had been defeated and the central focus of Jewish worship lay in ruins. By 135 CE, any remaining pockets of Jewish resistance had been crushed, the local Jewish population largely forced into exile, and the land of Judea renamed *Philistea*. How could Jewish life survive such a devastating setback? In fact, much of Jewish life didn't survive. Great numbers of Jews perished. The Temple's priests and Jewish sects such as the Sadducees and the Essenes receded from view or ceased altogether. However, two expressions of Jewish life did survive: one was to evolve into Judaism as we know it today. Rabbinic Judaism, a development of the religious impulse of the Pharisees and independent of the temple cult, advocated a form of "lay" religiosity that could be embedded in the everyday lives of the Jewish population. Domestic table rituals, Sabbath observance, the study of Torah, and the practice of deeds of loving kindness became the primary conscious focus of Jewish religious life in the absence of temple ritual (while incorporating the revered memory of the latter).

The other expression of Jewish life that was adaptable enough to survive the catastrophe was that practiced by followers of Jesus, and which would eventually develop into Christianity as we understand it today. Here, too, the religious life of the community was centered on word and table: an innovative interpretation of Israel's scriptures in the light of faith in the risen Christ and the early beginnings of eucharistic celebration. With this history in mind, scholars sometimes describe Judaism and Christianity as two "sibling" traditions rising from the ashes of the destroyed Jewish Temple. The roots of both lie in biblical Judaism. Over time, there evolved two distinct religious entities, what we know today as Judaism and Christianity. Scholars continue

TWELVE KEY THEMES

to study these developments that took place in the early centuries of the Common Era, with an ever-deepening appreciation of the complexity of the events and relationships that resulted in the so-called parting of the ways and the emergence of two self-defined religions.

Given this history, we can appreciate how deeply entwined is Christianity with the history and religious narrative of the Jewish people. But why should this matter now? Why would the Catholic Church of our time—through the teachings of Vatican II, of Pope John Paul II and his successors, and the repeated statements of curial documents—seek to draw attention to the Jewish roots of the church? It is because these roots are more than archaeological artifacts; they contain life-giving seeds that are necessary for the very life of the church and its continuing vocation. The biblical image of the olive tree (Rom 11:17–24) is helpful here. It features often in ecclesial documents that express the closeness of the relationship between Israel and the church. For example, speaking to a Jewish audience in 2009, Pope Benedict XVI said,

> Indeed, the Church draws its sustenance from the root of that good olive tree, the people of Israel, onto which have been grafted the wild olive branches of the Gentiles (cf. Rom 11:17–24). From the earliest days of Christianity, our identity and every aspect of our life and worship have been intimately bound up with the ancient religion of our fathers in faith.[2]

Let's name some of those Jewish roots upon which Christianity's origins and continuing vitality depend.

First, both traditions draw upon a common scripture, a text that tells the sacred story of ancient Israel and is

The Church Can Never Forget Its Jewish Roots

regarded by both traditions as revelation. Through the Hebrew Scriptures, God "speaks" to God's people, invites an encounter, and draws them close. Judaism is foundational to the Christian proclamation because the latter is built upon the divine authority of the Hebrew Scriptures. As stated by the Pontifical Biblical Commission, "Without the Old Testament, the New Testament would be an incomprehensible book, a plant deprived of its roots and destined to dry up and wither."[3]

Further, there is the spiritual heritage of Jewish prayer and ritual. Countless Christian ritual practices have Jewish antecedents. We could name, for example, the ritual cleansing associated with the waters of the Jewish *mikveh*, anointing with oil as a sign of sanctification and election, table rituals involving bread and wine, the psalms of the temple liturgy, the public readings from the Torah and the Prophets in the synagogue, prayers of remembrance and blessing, the practice of fasting, and so on. For as long as Christians turn to their sacred texts and treasure their liturgical and spiritual heritage, they will always encounter Jewish ancestors, Jewish beliefs, Jewish prayers, Jewish rituals, Jewish texts, Jewish traditions. They encounter "the rich root of the olive tree" (Rom 11:17).[4]

For Catholics and those churches defined by a sacramental tradition, a further way to appreciate the ongoing relevance of Christianity's Jewish roots is to ponder the *sacramentality* of the church. Christianity emerges from a religious experience that is not only experienced as enlightenment of the mind, but is anchored in the earthiness of the body, of history, of the "flesh and blood" realities of generational life. According to Christian faith, God has entered into the very fabric of human history. Jesus is not the result of religious "thought," he is the child born of a Jewish woman. He assumes her human nature as fully as he assumes the divine

TWELVE KEY THEMES

nature. Jesus is the Word "about" which scripture speaks, but, more deeply, he is the Word, "God's living Torah."[5]

Further, the Jesus whom Christians encounter in the Gospels is never an isolated individual; he is a member of a family, a community, a covenantal people steeped in the traditions of Israel that are passed down from parent to child. It is precisely within this matrix of Jewish relationships that Catholic doctrine understands the radical beginnings of the church. Whilst Jesus is the *source* of the church (Catholic doctrine holds that Christ "instituted" the church), Catholic teaching also considers Jesus' mother and the twelve apostles to be foundational figures to ecclesial existence. In the biblical narrative, Mary and the apostles are intimately involved in Jesus' life and mission. Jesus is savior, but not an isolated savior. He enters human history through the womb of a Jewish mother, physically and spiritually nurtured by her and her people and traditions; his ministry is intimately shared with an inner circle of companions. The figures of Mary and the apostles in subsequent church doctrines, prayers, and feast days enshrine this truth: the church, in its radical origins, is founded in loving relationships. By divine initiative the church is "birthed" through communion; it is not created by a human decision-making body or committee vote.[6] Viewed this way, how can the church ever be divorced from the Jewish relational bonds from which it sprang, from which the Christ himself came forth "according to the flesh" (cf. Rom 9:5)? Thus did the council fathers at Vatican II, pondering the depths of the mystery of the church, declare the people of the new covenant to be spiritually tied to "Abraham's stock" (*NA* 4).

In short, Jewishness matters. It mattered for Jesus, for Mary, for the apostles ("the Church's main-stay and pillars," *NA* 4). It is the ancestral relationship that grounds the deepest memory of the church. And it continues to matter for Christians today, compelled as they are to live their Christian vocation "in contact with its deepest tradition."[7] This is the recovered insight, which Vatican II discerned, which Christian scholars continue to study, and which God's people encounter over the course of their lives. We live in exciting times, evoking multilayered questions and much to ponder. As homilists and teachers, we may not always have the minutiae of the theological discussions at our fingertips, but at the very least we can confidently affirm the immense value and relevance of the Jewish roots of Christianity.

CHECKLIST FOR TEACHERS AND HOMILISTS

Do my listeners hear the Jewish roots of Christianity mentioned in my teaching or preaching? Or are they left with the impression that Christian beliefs and practices emerged "out of the blue" or were simply the "brainchild" of Jesus?

When I teach scripture, do I readily refer to and engage with the Hebrew Scriptures/Old Testament that comprise the greater portion of the Christian Bible? Or do I only attend to the New Testament?

When I teach about Christian liturgy, do I refer to its Jewish antecedents such as the practice of blessing, fasting, table rituals involving bread and wine, anointing with oil, ritual cleansing, the psalms of the temple liturgy, the proclamation of the scriptures in the synagogue, and so on?

When I discuss prayer and spirituality, do I mention, for example, the Jewish character of the

TWELVE KEY THEMES

    Our Father or the patterns of Jewish remembrance which underlie the eucharistic prayers of the Mass?

In communicating God's love for the church, do I also impart an awareness of God's beloved people, Israel, to whom the church looks for its spiritual ancestry, and the Jewish communities who continue to live and love and pray alongside the life of the church today? Or does my silence suggest to my listeners that Judaism is irrelevant?

3

GOD'S COVENANT WITH THE JEWISH PEOPLE IS ALIVE AND ACTIVE

KEY POINTS

This chapter explores a remarkable development in Catholic teaching that raises eyebrows and evokes searching questions, and yet is increasingly present in official ecclesial documents.

- Judaism is not an outdated, nullified, obsolete religion, and the church does not "replace" the Jewish people. Catholic teaching rejects this supersessionist view.
- The Catholic Church affirms the enduring vitality of Jewish covenantal life. The Jewish people are recognized as divinely called and loved by the faithful God who never breaks promises or revokes gifts (cf. Rom 11:28–29; *LG* 16; *NA* 4).
- God's covenant with Israel is "never revoked" (see Pope John Paul II's addresses at Mainz, 1980; Rome, 1986; Sydney, 1986; Sinai, 2000).
- Christian scholars continue to study these teachings in the light of the Christian proclamation of Jesus Christ, universal savior.

TWELVE KEY THEMES

NOTABLE ECCLESIAL TEXTS

Second Vatican Council

There is, first, that people to whom the covenants and promises were made, and from whom Christ was born according to the flesh (cf. Rom 9:4–5): in view of the divine choice, they are a people most dear for the sake of the fathers, for the gifts of God are without repentance (cf. Rom 11:28–29).

LG 16

Nevertheless, God holds the Jews most dear for the sake of their Fathers; He does not repent of the gifts He makes or of the calls He issues—such is the witness of the Apostle.

NA 4

Pope John Paul II

On November 17, 1980, Pope John Paul II addressed Jewish representatives at Mainz, Germany, where he acknowledged that the Jewish people are "the people of God of the Old Covenant, *never revoked* by God [cf. Rom 11:29]."[1]

Then again, on February 26, 2000, in the Year of the Great Jubilee, in an address at Mount Sinai, the Pope said, "But now on the heights of Sinai this same God seals his love by making *the covenant that he will never renounce.*"

And on November 26, 1986, in an address to Jewish community leaders in Sydney, the Pope reiterated, "For the Jewish people themselves, Catholics should have not only respect but also great fraternal love for it is the teaching of both the Hebrew and Christian Scriptures that the Jews are beloved of God, who has called them with an *irrevocable calling.*"

Catechism of the Catholic Church

The Old Testament is an indispensable part of Sacred Scripture. Its books are divinely inspired and retain a permanent value, for the Old Covenant has never been revoked.

CCC (1993), 121

Pope Francis

We hold the Jewish people in special regard because their covenant with God has never been revoked, for "the gifts and the call of God are irrevocable" (Rom 11:29). The Church, which shares with Jews an important part of the sacred Scriptures, looks upon the people of the covenant and their faith as one of the sacred roots of her own Christian identity (cf. Rom 11:16–18). As Christians, we cannot consider Judaism as a foreign religion; nor do we include the Jews among those called to turn from idols and to serve the true God (cf. 1 Thess 1:9). With them, we believe in the one God who acts in history, and with them we accept his revealed word.

EG 247

Pontifical Commission for Religious Relations with the Jews

That there can only be one history of God's covenant with mankind, and that consequently Israel is God's chosen and beloved people of the covenant which has never been repealed or revoked (cf. Rom 9:4; 11:29), is the conviction behind the Apostle Paul's passionate struggle with the dual fact that while the Old Covenant from God continues to be in force, Israel has not adopted the New Covenant.

"Gifts and Calling," 34

Pontifical Council for the Promotion of New Evangelization

The New Covenant does not replace God's Covenant with Israel, but presupposes it: that first Covenant has never been revoked (cf. Rom 11:28–29) and retains its validity, which finds complete fulfilment in that which Jesus accomplished with his mystery of salvation.

Directory for Catechesis, 348d

EXPLORING THE THEME

A most significant development in Catholic teaching today is the recovery and ever-deepening appreciation of the Pauline understanding that

> God loves the Jewish people,
> is faithful to that love,
> and has called Israel into a saving covenantal
>   relationship that remains unbroken,
>   unrepealed, unrevoked by God. (see Rom
>   11:28–29)

Echoing St. Paul, the Second Vatican Council taught that the Jews remain very dear to God, for the sake of

God's Covenant with the Jewish People Is Alive and Active

their fathers, since God does not take back the gifts divinely bestowed or the choice made.[2] Subsequent papal teachings and curial documents illuminate the significance of this statement, by speaking of the "irrevocable" Jewish covenant. The first explicit articulation of this later development is traced to Pope John Paul II. At Mainz, West Germany, in 1980, the pope spoke forthrightly of the Old Covenant as "never revoked." More than once in 1986 he referred to God's "irrevocable" calling of the Jewish people. In the Year of the Great Jubilee, 2000, standing at Mount Sinai, the traditional site of the God-given gift of the Mosaic law, he spoke of God's love for Israel as "the covenant that he will never renounce." This conviction has been reiterated in the public addresses of Pope Benedict XVI and Pope Francis, as well as in a number of Roman Catholic documents—including an apostolic exhortation, the *Catechism* and curial statements of the official Catholic-Jewish dialogue. It continues to be explored by theologians of the wider Jewish-Christian dialogue.

So why, you might ask, is this such an exciting development? Surely, the affirmation that God is faithful to divine promises is an obvious and unquestionable position for Catholic teaching! We Christians firmly place our trust in divine fidelity when we hear the words of Christ, "I am with you always" (Matt 28:20). And if God is faithful to the church, then God must also be faithful to Israel, God's "first love" (see Rom 1:16). To suggest that, with the coming of Christ, God has withdrawn the divine choice of Israel makes no sense. It effectively places in doubt God's fidelity and renders untrustworthy God's covenantal relationship with the church. If God can renege on the divine promise made to Israel, then who is to say God won't also abandon the church?

Yet, for centuries, a distorted message was too often communicated by generations of Christian homilists and

TWELVE KEY THEMES

teachers, even by certain great theologians and saints: Because the Jews did not accept Jesus as messiah and Son of God, they had somehow forfeited the gift of God's love and fidelity; because the Jews had rejected Jesus, God had rejected them. In fulfilling the Law, Jesus had rendered the Old Covenant obsolete; God's saving grace now rested with the predominantly gentile church—the "New Israel" had replaced the old. This latter statement has a descriptive term: *supersessionism*.

Even today, supersessionist views and other prejudicial sentiments continue to infiltrate Christian thought, albeit in milder forms. Jews might not be described as "rejected" by God, but they are seen as having "missed the boat" with Jesus; they are seen as continuing in their ignorance, lovingly tolerated and befriended by Christians, but their Jewish faith and traditions are regarded in some sense to be inadequate, misplaced, "second best" to Christianity. If we are honest, every Christian will find at least some variant of this thinking, however mild, in his/her personal faith journey. What every Catholic needs to know, then, is that their own church, along with other churches, has "dug deep" into the great tradition to rediscover and reinvigorate a profound, nonnegotiable truth: the Jews are the beloved of God, and God is relentlessly faithful. The God who has loved, called, liberated, and acted with Israel throughout history will never abandon this people, will never "downgrade" their calling to an inferior or "second-best" status. God's covenant with Israel is "never revoked," and this refers to the Jews of today as much as those of biblical times. Citing St. Paul, Vatican II asserted the scriptural foundation of this teaching, while Pope John Paul II led the way in making it explicit. Meanwhile, theologians and church leaders of stature, such as Cardinal Walter Kasper, have firmly endorsed it as a guiding principle among the many questions that bring Christians and Jews to the table of dialogue:

> One of these questions is how to relate the covenant with the Jewish people, which according to St. Paul is unbroken and not revoked but still in vigor, with what we Christians call the New covenant....The old theory of substitution is gone since the Second Vatican Council. For us Christians today the covenant with the Jewish people is a living heritage, a living reality. There cannot be a mere coexistence between the two covenants. Jews and Christians, by their respective specific identities, are intimately related to each other.... Such a question touches the mystery of Jewish and Christian existence...[3]

What, then, are we to make of our Christian faith conviction that Jesus is the New Covenant who "fulfills" the Old Covenant? Such statements are deeply embedded in our tradition, especially the liturgy. There is no suggestion here of negating their core truth. However, certain nuances in expression and interpretation are in order. "Fulfilled" in Christ does not equate with the demise of Judaism. The kingdom of God that Jesus announced and inaugurated is a "work in progress" from our earthly perspective. Looking toward the second coming of Christ, the church can legitimately acknowledge the role of Israel as relevant, essential, necessary to the unfolding mystery of God's saving design. God remains actively present with and in the Jewish people, who continue to bear the name of God to the world through the commitment and fruits of their covenantal life.

TWELVE KEY THEMES

This new, or renewed, affirmation of the enduring Jewish covenant by the church is a groundbreaking development in the history of Jewish-Catholic relations. Yet it also creates an apparent theological dilemma for Christian doctrine. If the Jewish people remain in a saving relationship with God, yet do not regard Jesus as their savior and as Son of God, then how are we to understand the non-negotiable Christian belief in the universal saving role of Jesus and his unique mediatorship for all? Catholic doctrine does not allow for a "two covenant" theory whereby some people are saved by Jesus and others are saved by some other mediating means without Christ. Christians believe that the work of Christ is efficacious for all; that the salvation of all people is ultimately through the work and person of Jesus Christ (even if by ways that are mysterious and hidden from clear view). This theological conundrum may be unsettling, but it also presents an exciting opportunity of self-discovery for the church today. It is sometimes said that Christians in the twenty-first century are wrestling with what is essentially the same theological dilemma St. Paul faced in the first century: As disciples of Jesus, we unashamedly proclaim Jesus to be the one and only Christ, the savior of all, yes! And this Christ is a son of the Jewish people who continue to live in covenant with God, a salvific covenant that has never been revoked, yes! How to reconcile this twofold yes theologically is the ongoing work of scholars. St. Paul grappled passionately with the meaning of the Jewish-Gentile relationship in the light of his unshakeable conviction that Christ had reconciled all peoples to himself, just as we are doing anew today from a very different standpoint in history. Paul never resolved his dilemma, and theologians today readily admit that the questions they wrestle with may find resolution in a future known only to God.

God's Covenant with the Jewish People Is Alive and Active

Given that these challenges relate to core Christian doctrine, it is understandable that some Catholics balk at this claim of the "never revoked" Jewish covenant. There is a concern that, in acknowledging the full force of God's commitment to the Jewish people, the Christian claim to salvation through Christ might in some way be compromised, undermined, diluted. We are, after all, historically accustomed to seeing ourselves as the "superior" religious entity over all others; a church that has the answer, right doctrine, and knows where it stands before God and amidst other world religions. Now we find ourselves having to turn to the Jewish people for insights, wisdom, and partnership in order to simply understand ourselves!

As uncomfortable as the teaching of the irrevocable covenant may be, it is difficult to see on what grounds this affirmation, growing in crescendo, could be reversed. Even those theologians who have recently urged caution and called for a more nuanced examination of this claim are prepared to admit that it has entered the teaching of the Catholic Church. In a 2018 reflection on the "never revoked covenant," Pope Emeritus Benedict XVI wrote, "It was pronounced for the first time by John Paul II on November 17, 1980, in Mainz. It has since been included in the *Catechism of the Catholic Church* (no. 121) and thus belongs in a certain sense to the current teaching of the Catholic Church."[4] Similarly, Catholic theologian Gavin D'Costa argues that, while the teaching of the "never revoked covenant" (understood as applying to present-day Jews) hasn't been formally ratified by an ecumenical council, it has been consistently taught for more than half a century since Vatican II, by the cumulative authority of three popes in their public speeches, by an apostolic exhortation and by the *Catechism of the Catholic Church*. In D'Costa's assessment, these "together account for an extension of the initial doctrine [of Vatican

TWELVE KEY THEMES

II]—a development of doctrine." However, the developed doctrine "has not yet attained a formal authoritative status but is on the road to that status."[5] Presumably this means that we can reasonably expect that God's irrevocable covenant with the Jewish people will be declared as such as part of a dogmatic constitution at a future Vatican III. In the meantime, while we Catholics sort out the intricacies of our doctrinal expressions, the Jewish people continue to live their life of covenant with God—often at great cost—as they have done for millennia.

We close this discussion with a question at the heart of our contemporary conversation. If theologians and bishops struggle with these intense theological questions, how on earth are Catholic teachers and homilists and parents meant to impart this church teaching to the young? Fortunately, they are not expected to have all the answers! However, as members of the faithful, we are all vital to the answer by the way we conduct our lives. We simply need to play our part responsibly in this unfolding development. What we *can* do with confidence is affirm the enduring vitality of Jewish covenantal life, knowing that we are treading in the footsteps of St. Paul, the Second Vatican Council, the public speeches of the three most recent popes, the *Catechism of the Catholic Church*, an apostolic exhortation, and curial statements arising from the Catholic-Jewish dialogue conducted by the Vatican in recent decades. We can safely reiterate, in the words of Pope Francis, quoting St. Paul, "We hold the Jewish people in special regard because their covenant with God has never been revoked, for 'the gifts and the call of God are irrevocable' (Rom 11:29)."[6]

At the same time, we can humbly acknowledge the very real questions this development of doctrine raises, not denying the challenges, but prayerfully and lovingly entering into this historic opportunity for deepened Christian self-understanding. Most of all, we can respectfully turn our hearts and minds toward actual Jews—neighbors, friends, colleagues, teachers, scholars, and leaders of Jewish communities. We can listen, learn, and revisit anew our own deeply held Christian convictions. Most of all we seek to *love* as God loves. In this way we will be participating in this historic and healing journey of ecclesial renewal. To close with the words of Pope John Paul II on his visit to Sydney in 1986: "For the Jewish people themselves, Catholics should have not only respect but also great fraternal love for it is the teaching of both the Hebrew and Christian Scriptures that the Jews are beloved of God, who has called them with an irrevocable calling."[7]

CHECKLIST FOR TEACHERS AND HOMILISTS

- In my teaching or preaching, is the point made clearly that "the Jews remain very dear to God" (*NA* 4; cf. Rom 11:28) and that acknowledgment of the enduring vitality of Jewish covenantal life is essential to an authentic Christian understanding of Judaism? Or is this denied or treated ambiguously?
- Do I impart an awareness of God's covenant with the Jewish people as the foundation of the new covenant? Do lessons or homilies make clear that God's covenant with the Jewish people was not nullified with the establishment of the new covenant in Christ? Or are my listeners left with the impression that the Jewish covenant has been rejected or annulled by God with the coming of Christ?

TWELVE KEY THEMES

Have I ever introduced my parishioners or students to statements from Catholic ecclesial documents that affirm God's irrevocable love for and call of the Jewish people (such as the ones quoted in this book)? Or have they never read or heard these statements?

God continues to love the Jewish people with an everlasting, steadfast love. Do my students or parishioners see God's love for the Jewish people reflected in me, through word and action?

4

THE OLD TESTAMENT IS FOUNDATIONAL TO THE NEW TESTAMENT

KEY POINTS

This chapter considers the relationship between the Old and New Testaments, and between the Jewish Scriptures and the Christian Bible.

> God's word is one single, undivided reality. The Catholic Church rejects any presumed opposition between the two Testaments.
>
> The Hebrew Scriptures are foundational to the Christian Bible. The New Testament is grounded in the divine authority of the Hebrew Scriptures. "Without the Old Testament, the New Testament would be an unintelligible book, a plant deprived of its roots and destined to dry up and wither."[1]
>
> The church interprets the Old Testament in the light of the New Testament (and vice versa). However, this does not preclude the Jewish Scriptures from holding meaning in their own right.

TWELVE KEY THEMES

Dialogue between Christians and Jews is to be encouraged, and can prove especially fruitful in the study of shared scripture texts. Christians can learn from Jewish exegesis.

NOTABLE ECCLESIAL TEXTS

Second Vatican Council

The plan of salvation foretold by the sacred authors, recounted and explained by them, is found as the true word of God in the books of the Old Testament: these books, therefore, written under divine inspiration, remain permanently valuable.

DV 14

Catechism of the Catholic Church

The Old Testament is an indispensable part of Sacred Scripture. Its books are divinely inspired and retain a permanent value, for the Old Covenant has never been revoked....

Christians venerate the Old Testament as true Word of God. The Church has always vigorously opposed the idea of rejecting the Old Testament under the pretext that the New has rendered it void (Marcionism).

CCC (1993), 121, 123

Pontifical Biblical Commission

Christians can and ought to admit that the Jewish reading of the Bible is a possible one, in continuity with the Jewish Sacred Scriptures from the Second Temple period, a reading analo-

The Old Testament Is Foundational to the New Testament

gous to the Christian reading which developed in parallel fashion. Each of these two readings is part of the vision of each respective faith of which it is a product and an expression. Consequently, they cannot be reduced one into the other.

On the practical level of exegesis, Christians can, nonetheless, learn much from Jewish exegesis practiced for more than two thousand years, and, in fact, they have learned much in the course of history.

> "The Jewish People and Their Sacred Scriptures in the Christian Bible," May 24, 2001, 22

Pope Benedict XVI

We must not forget that the Old Testament retains its own inherent value as revelation, as our Lord himself reaffirmed (cf. Mark 12:29–31). Consequently, 'the New Testament has to be read in the light of the Old. Early Christian catechesis made constant use of the Old Testament (cf. 1 Cor 5:-8; 1 Cor 10:1–11)" (*CCC* 128). For this reason the Synod Fathers stated that "the Jewish understanding of the Bible can prove helpful to Christians for their own understanding and study of the Scriptures."

> *VD* 41

Pope Francis

God continues to work among the people of the Old Covenant and to bring forth treasures of wisdom which flow from their encounter with his word. For this reason, the Church also is enriched when she receives the values of Judaism.

EG 249

Pontifical Commission for Religious Relations with the Jews

Judaism and the Christian faith as seen in the New Testament are two ways by which God's people can make the Sacred Scriptures of Israel their own. The Scriptures which Christians call the Old Testament is open therefore to both ways. A response to God's word of salvation that accords with one or the other tradition can thus open up access to God, even if it is left up to his counsel of salvation to determine in what way he may intend to save mankind in each instance. That his will for salvation is universally directed is testified by the Scriptures....Therefore there are not two paths to salvation according to the expression "Jews hold to the Torah, Christians hold to Christ." Christian faith proclaims that Christ's work of salvation is universal and involves all mankind. God's word is one single and undivided reality which takes concrete form in each respective historical context.

In this sense, Christians affirm that Jesus Christ can be considered as "the living Torah of God."

"Gifts and Calling," 25, 26

Pontifical Council for Promoting New Evangelization

The Old Testament is an integral part of the one Christian Bible, and the Church bears witness to

The Old Testament Is Foundational to the New Testament

> her faith in the one God who is author of both Testaments, thus rejecting any presumed opposition between the two.
>
> *Directory for Catechesis*, 348c

EXPLORING THE THEME

Let us begin this topic with a brief comment on the relationship between the Jewish Scriptures and the Christian Bible. Peruse the content of your Bible. You will notice that the majority of its pages are comprised of Old Testament texts. The Gospels and Epistles and other New Testament texts comprise a slim volume by comparison. Further, examine a timeline of the historical development of the books of the Bible. The relative recentness of the Christian New Testament will be strikingly obvious. Whereas the texts of the Old Testament emerged over the course of approximately a millennium, the New Testament writings emerged in the latter half of the first century of the Common Era.

What does this tell us? The Hebrew Scriptures (or Hebrew/Jewish Bible, the TANAKH[2])—that is, those sacred texts of ancient Israel that are recognized by Jews as divinely inspired scripture—are foundational to the one Christian Bible. This is true whether you are looking at a Protestant or Catholic or Orthodox version of the Bible. Certainly, there are notable differences between Jewish and Christian Bibles (we will discuss these in chapter 5). However, the point at hand is this: the New Testament authors presume as their frame of reference the scriptures of ancient Israel. The New Testament builds upon this foundation, interprets these Jewish texts, and introduces its own innovative proclamation as the basis of Christian faith. However, the New Testament does not, cannot, stand alone. It is profoundly

TWELVE KEY THEMES

linked to the Hebrew Scriptures and to the Jewish tradition that is the original custodian of those sacred texts.

The Hebrew Scriptures are foundational to the Christian Bible not only in terms of volume and chronology, but also in their theological significance as the revealed, and revealing, word of God.[3] This is a critical point in Catholic teaching that scholars of the Christian-Jewish dialogue bring to the fore of ecclesial consciousness: the New Testament presumes the divine authority of the Hebrew Scriptures. In order for the New Testament to be an encounter with the living word of God, the Old Testament must also bring us in contact with the living word of God. Put simply, for the new covenant to be authentic and truthful, the old covenant (the original covenantal relationship forged between God and the people of Israel) must also be authentic and truthful. The terms "old" and "new" here should be understood relatively as "first" and "second," "earlier" and "later;" there is no suggestion that what is first or earlier is outdated or obsolete. What comes later as the Christian proclamation of God's word depends upon and develops from what comes earlier as God's word spoken to Israel; and all this occurs within living communities of faith, responding to their religious memory as well as to the action of God in present events.

The Jewish texts that have been incorporated into the Christian Bible as the "Old Testament," then, should not be viewed simply as a "backdrop" to the Christian message. It would be inadequate to see the Old Testament as nothing more than a preparatory phase for the advent of Christ, to be read and then set aside while Christians occupy themselves with the New Testament. Rather, these Jewish Scriptures inform the very core of Christian self-understanding. Upon the witness of the Hebrew Scriptures, the Gospels depend.

The Old Testament Is Foundational to the New Testament

And lest we limit ourselves to thinking of these scriptures as "words on a page," church teaching (and scripture itself) reminds us that God's word is always a *living* word, embodied in the actual lives of people and communities; a word intimately bound to their relationships, ritual expressions, and traditions. In this context, we can appreciate how important is Christian awareness that Israel's Scriptures shaped the human experience of Jesus. These scriptures are an integral part of his earthly story that, from the standpoint of Christian faith, is a story inseparable from his personal identity as the Messiah and Son of God.

"Without the Old Testament the New Testament would be an incomprehensible book, a plant deprived of its roots and destined to dry up and wither."[4] Christianity would be lifeless were its roots not firmly planted in the earth of the Hebrew Scriptures. The church clearly grasped this in the early stages of its development when it ruled against the second-century heresy promoted by a certain bishop named Marcion. Marcion advocated that the Old Testament be discarded. Christianity, he reasoned, does not need this Old Testament God of wrath when it has the New Testament Jesus of love. He did not understand that to jettison the scriptures of Israel is to demolish the foundations of the New Testament.

Can we detect a hint of Marcionism still alive in our midst today? It is not uncommon to hear Christians refer to the so-called vengeful God of the Old Testament, while citing the verse "an eye for an eye." With the advent of the loving Jesus, a more loving and compassionate understanding of God is advocated by Christians, so the reasoning goes. As persistent and familiar as this line of thought is, it is not the teaching of the Catholic Church. Rather, Catholic teaching affirms that scripture forms a unity. The loving, liberating God to whom the Old Testament bears witness is

TWELVE KEY THEMES

the same God of love to whom the Gospels testify, albeit now revealed in the person of Jesus. Whilst the various textual layers of the biblical literature reflect their differing historical and cultural origins, authentic Christian interpretation does not drive a wedge between the two Testaments. This is a crucial point for educators, taught by *Dei Verbum* at the Second Vatican Council, and reiterated in the revised Vatican *Directory for Catechesis*, as indicated respectively in the following quotations:

> No less serious attention must be given to the content and unity of the whole of Scripture if the meaning of the sacred texts is to be correctly worked out.[5]

> The Old Testament is an integral part of the one Christian Bible, and the Church bears witness to her faith in the one God who is author of both Testaments, thus rejecting any presumed opposition between the two.[6]

What, then, are we Christians to make of the "difficult" passages of the Old Testament—those that speak of God's wrath, or even violence, toward human beings? We should approach them in the same way that we handle the difficult passages of the New Testament. For example, when we hear Jesus say to his disciples, "And if your right hand causes you to sin, cut it off and throw it away" (Matt 5:30), we interpret this not as a literal call for self-mutilation but as a figure of speech that finds its place in the message of scripture as a whole, appropriately interpreted within historical and literary contexts and the tradition of faith. What the church does with its difficult texts is also what Jewish communities do with their texts. Contextualized

The Old Testament Is Foundational to the New Testament

and interpreted in the light of their own religious experience, they know that the God of the Hebrew Scriptures is wholeheartedly faithful to Israel and to the good of humankind, is the God who never deals out justice without mercy, and who defends the honor of "the stranger, the orphan, and the widow."[7] Ethical principles of the highest order are forged through Jewish biblical reflection and form the basis of the church's own ethical system (we are familiar with the term "Judeo-Christian values"). To entertain the idea that the Jewish people are somehow less attentive to and less practicing of the love of God is a falsehood bound up with a reinvented strain of Marcionism. It devalues both the Hebrew Scriptures/Old Testament as the word of God and the Jewish people who are the bearers of God's Torah. In plumbing the scriptures, Jewish interpreters offer profound insights into the loving kindness and mercy of God; and these insights can benefit Christians in understanding more fully the person and teaching of the Jewish Jesus of the Gospels. One of the graces of the Second Vatican Council was that it called the Christian faithful to enter shared endeavors for the study of scripture with their Jewish counterparts, a practice that, where it occurs, is gradually dispelling the misunderstandings of the past and bearing fruit for people in both communities.

In recent decades, insights have emerged from the Jewish-Christian dialogue that point to further fruits and challenges to come for the church in its biblical education commitments. There was a time when Christians disparaged Jews for reading their scriptures without reaching the christological conclusions of Christianity. Further, many Christians placed value on the Old Testament only to the extent that it was seen to "foreshadow" the Christ-event. Today, however, the direction of scholarly reflection informed by the insights of the Jewish-Christian dialogue

TWELVE KEY THEMES

is highlighting that the Hebrew Scriptures hold validity and meaning *in their own right*, even without a Christian christological lens being brought to bear. Says the Pontifical Biblical Commission, speaking from an historical-critical perspective, "Christians can and ought to admit that the Jewish reading of the Bible is a possible one, in continuity with the Jewish Sacred Scriptures from the Second Temple period, a reading analogous to the Christian reading which developed in parallel fashion."[8] Each of these two ways of reading the biblical text is undertaken by a community of faith committed to reflecting on the word of God within the frame of its own established faith convictions. Thus, neither the Jewish nor the Christian reading can be reduced into the other. Both have legitimacy.

Drawing from common origins, and traveling side by side through history, there is an opportunity today for the Jewish and Christian readings to speak to and learn from each other. This opportunity, and challenge, is expressed as follows in the words of Pope Benedict XVI and Pope Francis, respectively:

> After centuries of antagonism, we now see it as our task to bring these two ways of rereading the biblical texts—the Christian way and the Jewish way—into dialogue with one another, if we are to understand God's will and his word aright.[9]

> God continues to work among the people of the Old Covenant and to bring forth treasures of wisdom which flow from their encounter with his word.[10]

This new opportunity for dialogue is encapsulated visually in a remarkable sculpture by Joshua Koffman,

Synagoga and Ecclesia in Our Time.[11] In this work, the two figures sit at the same level, side by side, turned toward one another as if engaged in dialogue (or in *havrutah*, a Jewish practice of Torah-study partnership). The Jewish figure holds the Torah scroll and the Christian figure holds the Christian Scriptures. They are distinct figures, yet the flow of their garments intermingle, perhaps suggesting a common purpose and unity in friendship. Without denying the significant differences that exist between Judaism and Christianity, Koffman's sculpture serves as a symbolic representation of a deepening realization among followers of Jesus that Christians can "learn much from Jewish exegesis practised for more than two thousand years, and, in fact, they have learned much in the course of history."[12]

CHECKLIST FOR TEACHERS AND HOMILISTS

- Are the texts of the Hebrew Bible/Old Testament presented as the living, dynamic word of God that continues to speak with spiritual vitality today? Or, do my listeners view them as a fossilized past and merely a preparatory stage for Christianity?
- Is the word *Old* in the term *Old Testament* understood to mean "ancient," "venerable," "first," "earlier"? Or do my listeners hear it as meaning "outdated," "superseded," "obsolete," "less important"?
- Do homilies or lessons acknowledge the Torah (Jewish Scriptures) as a source of inspiration for Jesus and the frame of reference for the New Testament authors? Or is the Torah viewed as

TWELVE KEY THEMES

a list of predictions fulfilled by Jesus, and no longer needed because Jesus has come?

Do I communicate to my students or parishioners that the Hebrew Scriptures are esteemed and hold validity in their own right? Or is the Old Testament undervalued and read only as a precursor to the New Testament?

Are my students or parishioners aware of the fruitful dialogue and shared Bible study projects that take place today between Jews and Christians? Or is it something that they never hear about?

5

CHRISTIANS AND JEWS ARE UNITED BY SCRIPTURE, BUT ALSO DIVIDED

KEY POINTS

This chapter continues the biblical focus of the previous chapter. Chapter 4 discussed the common ground of Christian and Jewish biblical perspectives. This chapter explores the differences.

- While Jews and Christians share a scripture, there are differences in the way their respective Bibles are structured and interpreted.
- The Catholic Church acknowledges the significant differences in textual interpretation, doctrine, and praxis that separate traditions, while welcoming friendly dialogue and exchange.
- Today, Christian scholars of the Jewish-Christian dialogue search for ways to better express Christianity's core message so as to reflect the integrity of both Jewish and Christian religious traditions, attentive to their commonalities and

TWELVE KEY THEMES

differences, and freed from the lingering effects of past anti-Jewish sentiment.

NOTABLE ECCLESIAL TEXTS

Second Vatican Council

The plan of salvation foretold by the sacred authors, recounted and explained by them, is found as the true word of God in the books of the Old Testament: these books, therefore, written under divine inspiration, remain permanently valuable. "For all that was written for our instruction, so that by steadfastness and the encouragement of the Scriptures we might have hope" (Rom 15:4).

DV 14

Pope John Paul II

May God allow Christians and Jews really to come together, to arrive at an exchange in depth, founded on their respective identities, but never blurring it on either side, truly searching the will of God the Revealer.

Such relations can and should contribute to a richer knowledge of our own roots, and will certainly cast light on some aspects of the Christian identity just mentioned. Our common spiritual patrimony is very large.

Address to Episcopal Conference Delegates of the Pontifical Commission for Religious Relations with the Jews, March 6, 1982

Christians and Jews Are United by Scripture

Pontifical Commission for Religious Relations with the Jews

That the Jews are participants in God's salvation is theologically unquestionable, but how that can be possible without confessing Christ explicitly, is and remains an unfathomable divine mystery. It is therefore no accident that Paul's soteriological reflections in Romans 9-11 on the irrevocable redemption of Israel against the background of the Christ-mystery culminate in a magnificent doxology: "Oh, the depth of the riches and wisdom and knowledge of God! How inscrutable are his judgments and how unsearchable his ways" (Rom 11:33).

"Gifts and Calling," 36

[The 2001 document of the Pontifical Biblical Commission] highlights that "Christians can learn a great deal from a Jewish exegesis practised for more than 2000 years; in return Christians may hope that Jews can profit from Christian exegetical research." In the field of exegesis many Jewish and Christian scholars now work together and find their collaboration mutually fruitful precisely because they belong to different religious traditions.

"Gifts and Calling," 44

Pope Benedict XVI

The text that follows is an excerpt from the Pope's personal theological study where he discusses the ancients' need to biblically interpret the catastrophic event of the destroyed Temple in 70 CE.

> One thing is clear: the Bible—the Old Testament—had to be read anew....There are two possible responses to this situation, two ways of reading the Old Testament anew after the year 70: the reading in the light of Christ, based on the Prophets, and the rabbinical reading....After centuries of antagonism, we now see it as our task to bring these two ways of rereading the biblical texts—the Christian way and the Jewish way—into dialogue with one another, if we are to understand God's will and his word aright.
>
> Joseph Ratzinger, *Jesus of Nazareth, Part Two, Holy Week: from the entrance into Jerusalem to the Resurrection* (San Francisco: Ignatius Press, 2011), 33–34

Pope Francis

While it is true that certain Christian beliefs are unacceptable to Judaism, and that the Church cannot refrain from proclaiming Jesus as Lord and Messiah, there exists as well a rich complementarity which allows us to read the texts of the Hebrew Scriptures together and to help one another to mine the riches of God's word.

EG 249

The Christian confessions find their unity in Christ; Judaism finds its unity in the Torah. Christians believe that Jesus Christ is the Word of God made flesh in the world; for Jews the

Christians and Jews Are United by Scripture

Word of God is present above all in the Torah. Both faith traditions find their foundation in the One God, the God of the Covenant, who reveals himself through his Word. In seeking a right attitude towards God, Christians turn to Christ as the fount of new life, and Jews to the teaching of the Torah. This pattern of theological reflection on the relationship between Judaism and Christianity arises precisely from *Nostra Aetate* (cf. no. 4), and upon this solid basis can and must be developed yet further.

Address to the International Council of
Christians and Jews, June 30, 2015

EXPLORING THE THEME

Jews and Christians share a common scripture. We discussed this in chapter 4, noting its significance for the Jewish-Christian relationship. In the shared texts through which God's word is encountered by both Jews and Christians, one finds the sacred story told of God's relationship with the people of Israel.

Further, the New Testament, while not recognized as Sacred Scripture within Judaism, depends upon the Hebrew Scriptures for its authority. The one who "fulfills" the covenant is a descendant of Abraham, son of David, the promised Messiah "according to the Scriptures" (see Luke 24:27; Acts 2). Without its basis in the authority of the Hebrew Scriptures/Old Testament, the New Testament could not testify to Christ. The Christian Bible's continuity with Israel's Scriptures is one compelling reason why the church sees itself as permanently related to the Jewish people.

TWELVE KEY THEMES

Christians, then, are linked to Judaism in their very identity. Pope John Paul II described the Jewish religion as "intrinsic" to Christianity, saying that with Judaism Christians have a relationship that they do not have with any other religion.[1] It is interesting to ponder this statement. Whilst in one sense the Jewish-Christian link can be described as an *interreligious* relationship, in another sense it is an *ecumenical* bond.[2] The first schism in the history of the church was not the one that resulted in estranged Christian churches, but rather the breakdown in relationship between emerging Christian communities and mainstream Judaism.

A further notable fact of history lies in the story of the Vatican's organizational processes. When Jewish-Catholic relations came to be added to the curial agenda in 1960, it was placed under the Secretariat for Promoting Christian Unity.[3] This was largely for practical reasons. After all, no secretariat for interreligious relations existed at the time. However, when the latter was established four years later, the Vatican's dialogue with the Jewish people remained under the ecumenical auspices and was not transferred to the Secretariat for non-Christians.[4] The decision to keep it within this ecumenical frame of reference stemmed from a theological rationale, not only from practical expediency.

Whilst affirming all that unites Christianity with Judaism, however, the focus of this chapter is to examine what *separates* the two as religious entities today. Acknowledgment of differences is as vital to honest, searching, respectful dialogue as is the affirmation of similarities. These differences are evident by examining the structure of the Bible itself.

To begin with, the number of books included as scripture differ between Jewish and Christian traditions. Several Jewish works that were not accepted into the canon

Christians and Jews Are United by Scripture

of the Jewish Bible (nor of Protestant Bibles) appear in the Old Testament of Catholic and Orthodox Bibles. Certain discrepancies in numbering conventions for chapters and verses reflect the fact that Christianity's early scriptural development followed the Septuagint, the ancient Greek translation of the Hebrew Scriptures.

Further, of those scriptures held in common by Jews and all Christian denominations, the ordering of books is not identical. This difference reflects theological outlook. Christian and Jewish Bibles all begin with the five books of the Torah/Pentateuch (Genesis, Exodus, Leviticus, Numbers, Deuteronomy). From there, the Jewish Bible (the TANAKH) proceeds with the prophetic books (*Nevi'im*) such as Isaiah, Jeremiah, Ezekiel, followed by the remaining writings (*Ketuvim*) such as the Psalms, Proverbs, Job.

In Christian Bibles, the prophets are placed later in the order of books. Those books of the Old Testament common to all Christian Bibles conclude with the prophet Malachi prophesying about the end-time. "Lo, I will send you the prophet Elijah before the great and terrible day of the Lord comes" (Mal 4:5). For the Christian interpreter, Malachi's words set the stage for the New Testament with Matthew's opening genealogy and the figure of John the Baptist, herald of the good news. The movement here is from prophetic utterance to its fulfillment in the birth of Jesus.

Meanwhile, the Jewish Bible concludes with a text from Second Chronicles anticipating the return of the Judean exiles to rebuild their homeland and exhorting the Lord's people to "go up" to Jerusalem. It, too, ends with a voice of hope-filled anticipation of a redemptive event, but with a different focus to its Christian counterpart.

In the previous chapter we emphasized the dependency of the New Testament on the Old Testament. Equally important is that Christians interpret their Old Testament

TWELVE KEY THEMES

in the light of the New Covenant. That is, Christians interpret the two Testaments in relation to each other. For Jews, however, there is no additional Testament. Their interpretative lens for reading the Hebrew Scriptures is the Oral Torah (the Mishnah, Talmud, and other non-scriptural sacred writings). Similarly, Catholics interpret their scriptures, as a whole, in the light of tradition (the teachings of church councils, the writings of the church fathers, the witness of the saints, and so forth).

The theological differences intensify. From the Christian faith perspective, God's word spoken through the scriptures of Israel culminates in an unsurpassed manner in Jesus Christ, the "Word made flesh." This faith conviction propelled a critical distancing movement for the church in its gradual separation from mainstream Judaism. Within several centuries, the formal articulation of Christian belief in Jesus as the Messiah and Son of God, as well as the doctrine of the Trinity, had set the two traditions apart. These weighty differences cannot be lightly glossed over. No matter how acceptable Jesus the Jew might be to sympathetic Jewish readings of the New Testament, at the end of the day the Christian claim concerning the unity of the divine and human natures in the person of Jesus is not acceptable to Judaism, which sees this as an affront to monotheist faith. This credal impasse shapes other differences in biblical sensibilities as well. Even appeals to a shared "Abrahamic heritage" can sometimes mask deep fissures in how Jews, Christians, and Muslims interpret the figure of Abraham.[5] Religious traditions can be so near to one another, and yet at the same time so far apart, depending on the window from which the religious landscape is viewed.

Doctrinal disagreement between Jews and Christians, however, should not lead to interpersonal antagonism, much less enmity and hatred. Thankfully, the practice of

Christians and Jews Are United by Scripture

Jewish-Christian dialogue today reveals the benefits that come from mutual listening and scholarly exchange.[6] One example touches the very nerve center of difference. In times past, the Jewish no to the messianic identity of Jesus was met with Christian condemnation. Christian scholars of the dialogue today, however, readily describe this no as a necessary christological corrective. That is, much of what Jews have said no to in centuries past has been a distorted representation of Jesus encountered in their contact with Christianity—such as a Christ who rejects the Jewish people, or a Christ stripped of his Jewish identity. Jewish repudiation of these false Christ-images is not only morally and theologically right, it has helped Christian scholars to find their way back to an authentic christological position; albeit not before terrible harm done to Jewish lives. We can appreciate why the processes of dialogue can be so sensitive.

Within the vastly improved, now friendly forums of dialogue today, Jewish perspectives continue to enrich Christian christological reflection. For example, there are both Jewish and Christian scholars researching Jewish messianic ideas in the Second Temple period that may have helped shape the christological perspectives of the early Jesus movement.[7] Shared research interests are an encouraging fruit of the post–*Nostra Aetate* era.

One of the central concerns of Christian theologians engaged in the dialogue today is the search for ways to better articulate Christianity's central vision so as to reflect the integrity of both Jewish and Christian religious traditions, freed from the conditioning of classical Christian anti-Judaism. For example, "fulfillment" terminology has been ubiquitous to Christian self-expression, and often linked to the erroneous idea that Judaism is obsolete. Today, Christian scholars attuned to the Jewish-Christian dialogue seek to understand the term *fulfillment* in ways that avoid any narrowing and "closing down" of the Christian narrative, but which instead favor an eschatological key that "opens up" to infinite mystery with a view to the eschaton (end-time). The latter approach holds potential for creating theological "space" for Jews to enter the discussion while holding fast to their Jewish faith convictions, for messianic hope is something that both Christians and Jews share.

Over the course of the dialogue, reputable Christian theologians have debated the merits of "one covenant" and "two covenant" theories. In recent years, the direction taken by the Pontifical Commission for Religious Relations has pointed away from "two covenant" approaches. The 2015 document of the CRRJ emphasizes the oneness of God's word, of God's people, and of God's covenants, while allowing for a two-part theological distinction between Israel and the Nations. In other words, within one overarching covenantal movement of grace in history, the people of Israel and the community of Christian disciples each relate to the one living God in distinct, yet related, ways. This does not solve the difficult questions at stake, but it does encourage a particular direction of pursuit for theological dialogue. The nuances here are subtle but important. On the one hand, we can legitimately observe that "Christian confessions find their unity in Christ; Judaism finds its unity in the Torah."[8] However, this is not to say that there are two separate paths to salvation or two words of God or two unrelated elected peoples. Christian faith proclaims Christ as the savior of all; his redemptive work has universal efficacy. The task of Christian theology today is to find a coherent way to express this truth in a way that does not undermine another deeply held truth sounding in circles of dialogue, scholarship, and official ecclesial statements: *the Jewish people remain in a saving covenant with God who is eternally faithful to them.* The challenge of reconciling these seemingly "competing" truths within a coherent theology is immense, and to date there is no scholarly consensus amid a variety of admirable, fruitful attempts at christological and ecclesiological formulations. In the meantime, the very act of reflection and dialogue in this regard has strengthened the growing movement toward Jewish-Christian partnership, reconciliation, and mutual respect.

CHECKLIST FOR TEACHERS AND HOMILISTS

- Are the substantial differences between Judaism and Christianity given due attention, in a respectful and timely manner as part of Christian teaching and interfaith dialogue forums? Or are they ignored and glossed over?
- Is the Catholic Church's participation in Jewish-Christian dialogue acknowledged as a genuine attempt to forge an authentic expression of the Jewish-Christian relationship and as a healing response to the anti-Jewish tendencies of the past? Or is it ignored or presented as a threat to Christian faith?
- Is the Jewish no to Jesus' messianic and divine identity viewed empathetically against the backdrop of a long history of Christian anti-Judaism? Or is it viewed as "lack of faith" or "blindness to the truth"?
- Are the Israelite/Jewish characters in the Hebrew Scriptures identified as positive models of faith

TWELVE KEY THEMES

(albeit humanly fallible)? Or is their infidelity and rebelliousness always stressed?

Are the prophets of the Bible seen as God's spokespersons who call the people to fidelity to the Torah covenant? Or as predictors of a future Christianity?

Are the prophetic writings understood as part of a tradition of self-criticism that should guide Christian self-appraisal? Or are they misused to suggest the failure of Jewish faith in contrast to Christian fidelity?

6

JUDAISM IS A PRESENT-DAY "LIVING TRADITION"

KEY POINTS

This chapter encourages Christian reflection on Judaism as a "living tradition" that actively contributes to the world and from which the church can learn and benefit.

- Present-day Judaism should not be equated with the Judaism of the Bible. Just as Christianity has developed over two millennia, so too has Rabbinic Judaism evolved over that time.
- For both Jews and Christians, the life of faith involves more than an intellectual grasp of credal positions; it involves living relationships and intergenerational commitments.
- Christians can be inspired and enriched through engagement with Jews and Judaism.
- Increasingly, Christians are encouraged to learn from Jewish Torah insights and to appreciate the wisdom contained in the vast corpus of post-biblical Jewish literature.

TWELVE KEY THEMES

NOTABLE ECCLESIAL TEXTS

French Catholic Bishops' Committee for Relations with Jews

The position taken by the Second Vatican Council should be considered a beginning rather than a final achievement. It marks a turning point in Christian attitudes toward Jews and opens a path, permitting us to take the exact measure of our task. The Council Statement bases itself on a return to Scriptural sources and breaks with the mentality of the past. It calls all Christians to a new vision of the Jewish people, not only on the level of human relations but also on that of faith. It is impossible, of course, to re-examine all at once the assertions and historical attitudes of the Church, maintained for many centuries. Christian conscience has initiated a process, however, to recall the Jewish roots of the Church. It is important that a beginning has been made, that all strata of the Christian people be reached, and that the course be pursued with honesty and energy.

> Statement by the French Bishops' Committee for Relations with Jews, April 16, 1973

Pontifical Commission for Religious Relations with the Jews

The existing links between the Christian liturgy and the Jewish liturgy will be borne in mind. The idea of a living community in the service of God, and in the service of men for the love of God, such as it is realized in the liturgy, is just as character-

Judaism Is a Present-Day "Living Tradition"

istic of the Jewish liturgy as it is of the Christian one. To improve Jewish-Christian relations, it is important to take cognizance of those common elements of the liturgical life (formulas, feasts, rites, etc.) in which the Bible holds an essential place.

"Guidelines," II

This concern for Judaism in Catholic teaching has not merely a historical or archeological foundation. As the Holy Father said..., after he had again mentioned the "common patrimony" of the Church and Judaism as "considerable": "To assess it carefully in itself and with due awareness of the faith and religious life of the Jewish people *as they are professed and practiced still today*, can greatly help us to understand better certain aspects of the life of the Church."

We must remind ourselves how the permanence of Israel is accompanied by a continuous spiritual fecundity, in the rabbinical period, in the Middle Ages and in modern times, taking its start from a patrimony which we long shared, so much so that "the faith and religious life of the Jewish people as they are professed and practiced still today, can greatly help us to understand better certain aspects of the life of the Church" (John Paul II, 6 March 1982).

"Notes," I.3, VI.1

Pope Benedict XVI

Christians ought to become more conscious of the depth of the mystery of the Incarnation in order to love God with all their heart, with all their soul and with all their might (cf. Deut 6:5). Christ, the Son of God, became flesh in a people, a faith tradition and a culture which, if better known, can only enrich the understanding of the Christian faith. Christians have come to this deeper understanding thanks to the death and resurrection of Christ (cf. Luke 24:26). But they must always be aware of and grateful for their roots. For the shoot grafted onto the ancient tree to take (cf. Rom 11:17–18), it needs the sap rising from the roots.

> Apostolic Exhortation *Ecclesia in Medio Oriente*,
> September 14, 2012, 21

[Despite the past hostility between Christians and Jews], the interplay between both communities over the centuries proved so fruitful that it contributed to the birth and expansion of the civilization and culture commonly known as Judeo-Christian.

> *Ecclesia in Medio Oriente*, 22

Pope John Paul II

The Ten Commandments are not an arbitrary imposition of a tyrannical Lord. They were written in stone; but before that they were written on the human heart as the universal moral law, valid in every time and place. Today, as always, the Ten Words of the law provide the only true basis for the lives of individuals, societies and nations.

Judaism Is a Present-Day "Living Tradition"

> Today as always, they are the only future of the human family.
>
> Homily at Mount Sinai, Egypt,
> February 26, 2000

EXPLORING THE THEME

A fascinating small detail of the teaching of *Nostra Aetate* at the Second Vatican Council is its use of the present tense when quoting St. Paul's words about his fellow Israelites: For "theirs *is* the sonship and the glory and the covenants and the law and the worship and the promises; theirs *are* the fathers and from them *is* the Christ according to the flesh" (Rom 9:4–5), the Son of the Virgin Mary.[1]

In this conciliar statement we hear an affirmation that finds increasing emphasis as the Christian-Jewish dialogue proceeds, namely, that Jewish covenantal life is a present-day reality. Judaism is not an obsolete religion fading into the mists of history; Jewish community life and its traditions remain alive and active in the world. Thus, Catholic engagement with Judaism can never be reduced to historical or archaeological interest; the church is interested in a *living* relationship with *living* Jews.

Historical perspective is called for here. Sound scholarship and Catholic ecclesial documents distinguish between the Judaism of the Bible and Rabbinic Judaism. The latter is the expression of Judaism that developed in the period following the destruction of the Jewish temple in 70 CE (discussed in chapter 2). If Christians are to relate to Jews of today, they must understand that, while Judaism today is in continuity *with* the Bible, it is not the Judaism *of* the Bible. We cannot simply read the texts of the Old Testament and presume to know what Jews think, believe, or do in the twenty-first century. Just as Christianity has evolved since the time of Jesus and the emergence of the New Testament, so has Judaism undergone two millennia of development in that same time period. Further, the passage of time has seen fracturing disagreements resulting in denominational divisions within religions. Within Christianity we are familiar with Christians who identify as members of Orthodox churches, Catholic churches, Anglican, Baptist, Lutheran, Methodist and Reformed churches, as well as United and Independent churches. Similarly, today we find Jews identifying according to a number of expressions of Judaism, the three major streams being Orthodox, Conservative, and Reform, but with subgroupings such as Modern Orthodox and Haredi, and smaller streams such as Reconstructionist Judaism and Jewish Renewal, as well as Jews who describe themselves as "secular" Jews or "traditional" Jews or "just Jewish." Achieving unity amidst diversity is a perennial challenge for every religious tradition, as it is for every family and human society that values freedom and development.

What does it mean to be a "living tradition"? Let's take a moment to dwell upon this. Like Christianity and the church, Judaism and the Jewish people are defined by more than sacred texts and religious rituals. To be an observant Jew is to be a member of a living, breathing, active community of people, holding fast to ancient stories and ancestral traditions that speak of their relationship with the eternal God, while living the truth of those stories and traditions in and through the rhythms of Jewish life and the concrete events, relationships, and time-conditioned realities of the world in which they dwell. Sacred texts and rituals only make sense within this relational context.[2] In many respects, Catholic Christians can recognize in Jewish life their own religious dynamic.

Judaism Is a Present-Day "Living Tradition"

Further, authentic Christian engagement with Jewish communities and their traditions "can greatly help us to understand better certain aspects of the life of the Church."[3] This assertion invites the question: *How* can a living connection with Jews and Judaism positively impact Christian life today? What happens when Christians attune their ears, eyes, and hearts to God's continuing presence in Jewish families and communities? Time and again the testimony of those who have accepted this invitation can be heard as saying,

> *When we listen to Jews interpreting Torah, our own Christian biblical sensibilities are sharpened and expanded.*
>
> *When we become aware of Jews relating to God and one another through their annual cycle of holy days, our own passage through the Christian liturgical calendar is viewed with new eyes and experienced afresh.*
>
> *When we see Jews engaging in acts of loving kindness and humanitarian works guided by high ethical standards, we are inspired, challenged, and reassured that our Christian efforts have sure interreligious partnership in the service of God and the common good.*
>
> *When we come in contact with Jews covenanting with God through the joys and struggles of familial and community life, and reflect upon its meaning, we are brought closer to the person of the Jewish Jesus.*

This last point is particularly thought-provoking and paradoxical when one considers that there are some things about Jesus that are more immediately intuited by Jews

TWELVE KEY THEMES

than by Gentile Christians! A love for Torah, robust debate in its interpretation, the joy of Jewish festivals, a palpable connection with the "sacred time" of Sabbath, a sense of being present at Sinai, tears shed over Jerusalem...there are moments when Christians discover that their Jewish friends understand better than they do what makes Jesus "tick" as a Jew, for they can identify with the ancestral story of Jesus in a way that a Gentile does not, and cannot. We need not be surprised or threatened by this. It takes nothing away from the "inside" experience of being a Christian believer in relationship with the risen Jesus. For both Jewish and Christian religious experience entails more than knowing "about" one's credal position; it involves daily immersion in living relationships and intergenerational commitments. The resilience of Jewish families and kinship ties is one of the admirable features of Jewish life. If a Jewish friend can offer a Gentile Christian an insight into the heart of the Jew Jesus, it is because that friend knows, loves, and is "familied" to other Jews. But this must also be true of Jesus. In accord with his own earthly story as a faithful Jew, Jesus must also know, love, and be "familied" to other Jews.[4]

This last point brings a spiritual and psychological lens to Christian reflections on Judaism as a "living tradition." Think about it: If the Jesus of history was profoundly "familied" within a Jewish milieu, surely this must be a consideration in the way we Christians relate to Jesus in resurrection and glory. Put a different way: could we ever imagine Jesus, the divine Love Incarnate, ceasing to love and identify with his own Jewish kin, from whom he was born "according to the flesh"? Most observant Catholics have little difficulty imagining the risen and glorified Jesus with a special place in his heart for his mother, Mary, and his foster father, Joseph. Why should we be any less able to

Judaism Is a Present-Day "Living Tradition"

imagine a special place in Jesus' heart for every other Jewish relative or friend of his, and for his people as a whole whom scripture repeatedly depicts as God's beloved, Israel? Pushing this thought further, have we ever made a connection between the Feast of the Sacred Heart and the humanity of Jesus with a heart beating with love for his Jewish kin?[5] Or does Jewish identity simply "dissolve" or "disappear" into Christian claims about God loving "everyone"? Reflections like these, thoroughly Catholic, draw us to the heart of the Jewish Jesus and indicate how important Jewish influence is on the lives of Gentile Christians. As Pope Francis has said, "Dialogue and friendship with the children of Israel are part of the life of Jesus' disciples."[6]

Another way to appreciate the present-day relevance of Jewish life for Christian faith is to dwell on those scriptures held in common by Jews and Christians. A remarkable dimension of the Catholic-Jewish dialogue today is a deepening awareness within the church that the Jewish way of reading scripture is a valid reading. Whereas once most Christians assumed the Jewish interpretation to be flawed when it did not result in recognition of Jesus as messiah and Son of God, today there is a growing understanding that the Jewish reading is reasonable and valid, in two senses:

First, the Jewish reading is an authentic reading from a historical-critical perspective. The writings of the Old Testament came into being long before the time of Jesus. These texts express the faith of the people of Israel of those times and have a religious coherence within that context. For example, the Isaiah texts that speak of a "suffering servant" of God are rightly understood in the context of their time of composition as referring to an individual who represents the collective suffering of Israel. It is true that Christians read later events back into those texts and retroactively view the suffering servant as pointing to the future sufferings of Christ. This is the perspective of Christian faith. From a strict historical-critical perspective, however, the Isaiah texts could not have described events that hadn't yet occurred. Therefore, the original reading, elaborated by Jewish commentators over subsequent centuries, remains reasonable, coherent, valid, and does not contradict or take away from the Christian interpretation.

Second, scripture is not an isolated or abstract word; it does not exist apart from its embodiment in the lives of people of faith and their faith communities. When Catholics and other Christians turn to their Sacred Scriptures and liturgy, they discover there a *living* word, interpreted in "a living community in the service of God,"[7] and this is true of Jewish communities as much as Christian communities. Christians can therefore appreciate that the Jews as a people, who over time and still today *live* Torah as much as read and study Torah, remain the traditional custodians of these texts. Their relationship with Torah has never ceased or abated, for the Jewish people themselves, to this day and despite all opposing forces, continue to live and cherish and pass on the Torah and its related traditions.

Pope John Paul II put it this way: he spoke of a first and second dimension of Jewish-Christian dialogue. The first dimension is "the meeting between the people of God of the Old Covenant, never revoked by God [cf. Rom 11:29], and that of the New Covenant." Within our church this is a dialogue "between the first and the second part of her Bible." The Pope then went on to say, "A second dimension of our dialogue—the true and central one—is the meeting between present-day Christian Churches and the present-day people of the Covenant concluded with Moses."[8] In other words, an encounter with Sacred Scripture is more than an encounter with the Jews who fill the pages of scripture; it

Judaism Is a Present-Day "Living Tradition"

is also and always a living encounter with those Jews who bear, embody, and interpret those sacred texts today and in each new generation. A sense of scripture as "living word" flows organically with a central tenet of Christian belief: Jesus is the living Word of God; "the Word became flesh and lived among us" (John 1:14). This conviction is expressed anew in the theological writings of Joseph Ratzinger (Pope Benedict XVI) where he describes Jesus as "God's living Torah," a phrase that has entered the discussion and documents of the Catholic-Jewish dialogue.[9]

Another way to appreciate Judaism as a "living tradition" is to remember its historical development alongside Christianity. The early communities comprised of Jewish and Gentile followers of Jesus gradually came to define themselves as an identifiable religious entity, "Christianity," during a centuries-long process of parting from Jewish origins. In this journey, Jewish influence on emerging Christianity was felt through the influence of the Hebrew Scriptures; but it was felt in other ways as well. For example, scholars today explore how the New Testament was shaped not only by the Hebrew Scriptures but also by prominent nonbiblical Jewish ideas circulating in the centuries "between" the two Testaments. Ideas about the afterlife, messianism, judgement, and the end-time—expressed in ancient nonbiblical texts—found their way into the thought and writings of the New Testament authors.[10] Even after the Epistles and Gospels emerged, the exchanges between mainstream Jews and Jewish and Gentile Christ-followers continued to influence the development of their respective communities, within their shared cultural settings.

Further, beginning around 200 CE, the oral interpretative traditions of Judaism, including those that likely shaped communities in the time of Jesus, came to be written down to comprise a formidable corpus of Jewish

TWELVE KEY THEMES

religious literature. These texts include the Mishnah, the Gemarah, the Talmud. Added over time were the works of later commentators and scholars like Rashi, Maimonides, and Nachmanides. Generation after generation, layer upon layer, the intellectual, moral, and spiritual vitality of these writings is unquestionable in the world of Judaism.[11] But what do they mean for Christians? In centuries past, Christian authorities were known to ignore, disparage, oppose and even burn Jewish texts, regarding them as heresy and a threat to the church. An altogether different situation exists today where Christian theologians, in dialogue with Jews, are asking searching questions about the relevance of these Jewish works for Christian reflection. Given the scriptural links between Jews and Christians, and the interpenetrating influence of the two communities in the early centuries of the Common Era, can Christians simply ignore nonbiblical Jewish religious texts? If the Jewish people draw on these texts as part of their Torah interpretation and their Torah-observant lives, cannot the church, which is intimately bound to this Torah-bearing people, also profit from these nonbiblical Jewish writings in service of the word of God?

Questions and explorations like these within the Catholic community are indicative of an ever-growing recognition of the present-day vitality of the Jewish covenant and the church's willingness to engage with Judaism as a living, active, evolving tradition. Whilst homilists and teachers may not always be in a position to unpack the details of scholarly questions for their audiences, they are well placed to communicate a healthy respect for Judaism as a *living tradition*. In the words of Cardinal Walter Kasper, President of the Pontifical Council for Promoting Christian Unity (2001–10):

Judaism Is a Present-Day "Living Tradition"

Judaism is not a mere social and historical feature, but also a theological and current reality. God's Covenant with Israel has not simply been replaced by the new Covenant. God has not rescinded his contract with Israel; [God] has not repudiated and forsaken his people. Israel is still God's partner. God is still devoted to his people with love and loyalty, mercy, justice and pardon; God is always with his people especially in the most difficult moments of history. Every Jew, as one of [God's] people, lives in promise.[12]

CHECKLIST FOR TEACHERS AND HOMILISTS

Are Jews and Judaism discussed outside the biblical context? For example: Are students and parishioners aware of the vast body of Jewish sacred writings and scholarly knowledge forged after the time of Jesus (e.g., the Mishnah, the Talmudic writings, the commentators of later generations)? Or do students/parishioners have the impression that Judaism goes no further than the Hebrew Bible/Old Testament?

Are Jews mentioned in lessons about history in terms of their contributions (as can be seen in the intellectual contributions of modern Jewish thinkers such as Einstein, Levinas, Buber, Heschel, Sacks and others)? Or are they presented only as victims of persecution?

Are students or parishioners aware that, like Christianity, Judaism has evolved over time and today exists in diverse expressions?

TWELVE KEY THEMES

Or are contemporary Jews treated as a one-dimensional collective?

Are present-day Jewish communities remembered by Christian communities over the course of the liturgical year (e.g., in the prayers of the faithful) as Jews celebrate their festivals, some of which have historical/biblical links to Christian liturgical dates? Or does our Christian year unfold with rare or no mention of what is occurring in the Jewish calendar?

7
SCRIPTURE IS TO BE INTERPRETED WITHOUT ANTI-JEWISH BIAS

KEY POINTS

This chapter addresses the long history of anti-Jewish interpretation of scripture and how it continues to have a conditioning effect on present-day Christians.

- Even today, Christians are prone to unintended misuse of certain biblical texts and motifs in ways that undermine Jews and Jewish traditions, perpetuating certain caricatures that do harm to human dignity and to religious integrity.
- Particular vigilance is required when dealing with scriptural texts as part of the liturgy and in dramatizations of the passion narratives.
- Historical-critical scholarship provides essential insights for Christians reading scripture. For example, the person and teaching of Jesus are properly interpreted within the contextual framework of first-century Judaism. So, too, with St. Paul.

TWELVE KEY THEMES

The teaching of *Nostra Aetate* also frames the way Catholics today approach scripture vis-à-vis Judaism.

NOTABLE ECCLESIAL TEXTS

Second Vatican Council

What happened in His passion cannot be charged against all the Jews, without distinction, then alive, nor against the Jews of today. Although the Church is the new people of God, the Jews should not be presented as rejected or accursed by God, as if this followed from the Holy Scriptures.

NA 4

French Catholic Bishops' Committee for Relations with Jews

It is wrong to oppose Judaism as a religion of fear to Christianity as one of love. The *Shema Yisrael*, the fundamental article of Jewish faith begins: "You shall love the Lord your God," followed by the commandment to love one's neighbor (Lev 19:18). This is also the point of departure for Jesus' preaching, and therefore, a doctrine common to Judaism and Christianity.

"Statement by the French Bishops' Committee for Relations with Jews," April 16, 1973, IV, c

Scripture Is to Be Interpreted without Anti-Jewish Bias

Pontifical Commission for Religious Relations with the Jews

With respect to liturgical readings, care will be taken to see that homilies based on them will not distort their meaning, especially when it is a question of passages which seem to show the Jewish people as such in an unfavorable light. Efforts will be made so to instruct the Christian people that they will understand the true interpretation of all the texts and their meaning for the contemporary believer....

The Old Testament and the Jewish tradition must not be set against the New Testament in such a way that the former seems to constitute a religion of only justice, fear and legalism, with no appeal to the love of God and neighbor (cf. Deut 6:5; Lev 19:18; Matt 22:34–40).

"Guidelines," II, III

Jesus shares, with the majority of Palestinian Jews of that time, some pharisaic doctrines: the resurrection of the body; forms of piety, like alms-giving, prayer, fasting (Matt 6:1–18) and the liturgical practice of addressing God as Father; the priority of the commandment to love God and our neighbor (Mark 12:28–34). This is so also with Paul (Acts 23:8), who always considered his membership of the Pharisees as a title of honor (Acts 23:6; 26:5).

TWELVE KEY THEMES

Paul also, like Jesus himself, uses methods of reading and interpreting Scripture and of teaching his disciples which were common to the Pharisees of their time. This applies to the use of parables in Jesus' ministry, as also to the method of Jesus and Paul of supporting a conclusion with a quotation from Scripture.

"Notes," III.17–18

Arising from the same soil, Judaism and Christianity in the centuries after their separation became involved in a theological antagonism which was only to be defused at the Second Vatican Council....A replacement or supersession theology which sets against one another two separate entities, a Church of the Gentiles and the rejected Synagogue whose place it takes, is deprived of its foundations. From an originally close relationship between Judaism and Christianity a long-term state of tension had developed, which has been gradually transformed after the Second Vatican Council into a constructive dialogue relationship.

"Gifts and Calling," 17

Pope John Paul II

In the Christian world—I am not saying on the part of the church as such—erroneous and unjust interpretations of the New Testament relative to the Jewish people and their presumed guilt cir-

Scripture Is to Be Interpreted without Anti-Jewish Bias

culated for too long, engendering sentiments of hostility toward this people.

Address to Participants in the Vatican Symposium on "The Roots of Anti-Judaism in the Christian Milieu," October 31, 1997

EXPLORING THE THEME

In circles of Jewish-Christian dialogue we often hear about the problem of "supersessionism." What is supersessionism?

The term *supersessionism*, as it has come to be used in circles of Jewish-Christian dialogue today, refers to a distorted Christian interpretation of scripture that undermines the integrity of Judaism. According to a supersessionist view, because Christ has fulfilled the Old Testament promises, the people of Israel have been "superseded" and replaced by the church. It is a view that leads to a judgment upon Judaism as being an outdated religion, considered obsolete after the proclamation of the gospel of Jesus Christ in the apostolic period. Whilst supersessionism has been rife in Christianity for most of its history, it has never been officially taught as doctrine.[1] Following the Second Vatican Council, Catholic teaching has sought to arrest the spread of supersessionist ideas and to correct the misunderstandings they have spawned in the lives of the faithful.

We must nuance our comments here, for it can be argued that "supersession" also has a benign expression. One could point to supersessionism in the Bible itself, where certain covenantal moments give way to a further covenantal development as part of the unfolding relationship between God and Israel. For instance, God's covenant with Noah

TWELVE KEY THEMES

is a progressive development of the covenant with Adam and Eve; and, compared to God's covenant with Abraham, the Mosaic and Davidic covenants are further stages in the God-Israel relationship. The later voices of Israel's prophets that speak of a "new covenant" are another development again. However, as Harvard scholar Jon Levenson points out, whereas Jewish tradition has always esteemed the prior covenantal moment without seeking to disparage or undermine its significance, Christian commentary has a long history of downgrading the Jewish covenant in order to proclaim the new covenant of Jesus Christ.[2] It is through the studies and writings of French-Jewish historian Jules Isaac (1877–1963) that the term *supersessionism* enters the vocabulary of Jewish-Christian dialogue circles in the mid-twentieth century. In a careful study of the term in Isaac's work, Matthew Tapie points out that "supersessionism" is not simply *any* form of anti-Judaism (although it is often reinforced by other forms of anti-Judaism); precisely, supersessionism is the view that *because* Jesus fulfills the Law, *therefore* Judaism is finished, obsolete, and the people of Israel is replaced by the church.[3]

It is necessary to distinguish between the two parts of this definition. The first part states that Christians believe that Jesus Christ "fulfills" the promises of the covenant in the Old Testament Scriptures. This is in keeping with accepted Catholic teaching, noting, however, that the church has never settled upon any one particular form of fulfillment theology. It is *not* true to conclude that "fulfillment" in Christ is simply the "end of the story" and that there is nothing left to be accomplished in history by human beings. Nor is it true to conclude that this fulfillment does away with any need for Jews and Judaism. (History has proved such a view to be outright dangerous when one con-

Scripture Is to Be Interpreted without Anti-Jewish Bias

siders the slippery slope between declaring Judaism to be "finished" and viewing Jewish lives as expendable.) As we saw in chapter 3, Catholic teaching today affirms the dignity and enduring validity of Jewish covenantal life, and views Jewish communities as playing a continuing role in the unfolding of the divine plan in history. In the words of Pope John Paul II, God's covenant with the Jewish people is "never revoked." *How* Catholics express their claim about fulfillment in Christ, then, is vitally important lest they end up undermining both Jewish covenantal life and their own orthodoxy as Catholics.

We might be surprised to learn that, despite the healing journey begun at the Second Vatican Council, subtle supersessionism and other attitudes that undermine Judaism are still quite common among Catholics, and other Christians, today. Typically, they arise not through any conscious prejudice or intended malice, but from unintended faulty assumptions that overlook historical context and the nuances of the biblical text. Examples of common misperceptions that have supersessionist or anti-Jewish overtones include the following black-and-white contrasts:[4]

> Judaism of Jesus' day was nothing but harsh legalism, so Jesus freed people by preaching the law of love.
> All Pharisees were judgmental; their God was a severe judge, but Jesus revealed a different God, of mercy and compassion.
> Women in ancient Jewish society were given no rights or respect and were relentlessly oppressed, but Jesus was the ultimate feminist.
> Jews were preoccupied with purity laws that kept them segregated from "the unclean" at the

TWELVE KEY THEMES

expense of mercy and compassion, but Jesus overcame Jewish purity-based barriers and showed love to those rejected as "unclean."

Temple practices of Jesus' time amounted to nothing but oppression of the poor and outcasts who could not comply with ritual demands, but Jesus did away with the Jewish cult.

Jewish culture was insular, narrow-minded, exclusionary, xenophobic; Jesus reached out to all.

St. Paul was a bad, hateful Jew who, after his conversion experience on the road to Damascus, became a good, loving Christian. The legalism of the Jewish Law enslaved people, but St. Paul preached a covenant based on freedom in the spirit and grace of Christ.

These kinds of statements involve one or more of the following problems.

First, they overemphasize the limitations and faults of first-century Jewish society and underemphasize the nuances of the biblical evidence. For example, while the temple system in Jesus' day no doubt had its problems of political compromise, in scripture we also find Jesus and his disciples readily participating in temple worship; while Jesus surely had enemies among Pharisees, we also find in the New Testament Pharisees who were not opposed to Jesus—some welcomed him and warned him of danger; while gender equality in the first century was a far cry from what we would expect today, we also find in scripture female biblical figures speaking, initiating, and moving about freely (including those women who supported Jesus' ministry out of their own resources); and we find the matriarchs and

Scripture Is to Be Interpreted without Anti-Jewish Bias

other great women of the Hebrew Scriptures revered in Jewish tradition.

Second, the problematic statements listed above involve sweeping generalizations that fail to recognize the variety and creativity of Jewish expression. Likely, there was no single Jewish view about Sabbath, dietary laws, and messianic expectations in New Testament times, but rather plenty of contrasting opinions that reflected a lively pluralism in Jewish thought and practice. Paula Fredriksen, a scholar of early Christianity, offers the image of Torah as widely dispersed sheet music: "The notes were the notes, but Jews played a lot of improv."[5] The Gospels' depiction of the polemics between Jesus and other Jews may well reflect this rich diversity of Jewish belief and praxis.

Third, the statements listed above depict Jesus and Paul as standing *against* their Jewish tradition rather being involved in intra-Jewish complexities and debates. When their words and actions are interpreted without attention to their Jewish milieu, they can be heard as making anti-Jewish judgements. When we listen to Jesus and Paul speaking as Jews and operating from first-century Jewish assumptions, a different picture begins to emerge that is more congruent with Judaism. We must remember that followers of Jesus in New Testament times represented a numerically small, evolving expression of Jewish religious experience, attracting Jewish and then Gentile adherents; Judaism and Christianity were not two separately established religions as we think of them today. This is particularly relevant to the letters of St. Paul that deal with categories of "law" and "grace." These have often been misinterpreted by importing later intrachurch debates of the Protestant Reformation, debates that of course were unknown at the time of St. Paul. In recent decades a new area of Pauline scholarship ("the new perspective" on Paul)

TWELVE KEY THEMES

has challenged a number of long-standing Christian interpretations of Pauline texts and invited fresh appraisals of Paul, his mission and message.[6]

Fourth, the statements listed above fail to recognize that the Gospels may contain hostile references that reflect social and political conflicts that were occurring in the latter half of the first century. When we hear negative overtones given to "the Jews" it is wise to recall that the author is likely grappling with social and religious questions emerging decades after the time of Jesus (e.g., the question of how to respond to the influx of Gentiles into the Jewish-based Jesus movement). Often times, the words placed on the lips of Jesus and his contemporaries are likely shaped by the theological intentions of later writers rather than being a moment-by-moment record of what was said or done during the earthly lifetime of Jesus.

Fifth, these views often display a lack of understanding of how Jews themselves have interpreted their own texts and traditions over time. This is particularly true when it comes to references to temple sacrifice and purity laws—topics that are complex for informed Jews let alone Christian readers unfamiliar with Jewish practices. Care is needed, therefore, to understand such references with the help of Jewish knowledge, experience, and interpretative insights.

Finally, supersessionist readings of the Bible suffer from a lack of awareness of *Nostra Aetate* that sought to address a long history of anti-Jewish sentiment. They are unaware of the church's transition from a "teaching of contempt" to an overarching teaching of respect, reconciliation, dialogue, and solidarity in the way Christians relate to Jews. The challenge for Christians is to listen more carefully, for example, to how certain stock homiletic phrases or classroom comments might be heard by Jewish ears:

Scripture Is to Be Interpreted without Anti-Jewish Bias

respectful or denigrating? Acknowledging or dismissive? Loving or hurtful?

Lively discussions about supersessionism—its precise meaning, manifestations, causes, and remedy—continue in the Jewish-Christian theological dialogue of our time.[7] Scholars differentiate between varieties of supersessionism, with labels such as "hard," "soft," "punitive," "economic," and "structural" supersessionism. There are scholars who argue that some form of soft supersessionism is necessarily inbuilt to Christianity, because Christ will always be seen by his followers as the "fulfillment" of the promises of the Hebrew Scriptures. Others point out that what is at fault is our Christian conception of fulfillment, so conditioned by centuries of supersessionism that we struggle to envisage a new way of theologizing that fully respects the Jewish covenant. The discussion is ongoing, fascinating, at times, tense, but usually fruitful. Understandably, teachers and homilists may not always be cognizant of the technicalities of scholarly debates, however they can be alert to the more obvious misconceptions listed above and help guide their audiences in overcoming unintended anti-Jewish prejudice.

One of the most difficult places to address supersessionism and (unintended) anti-Judaism is liturgical celebration. Within the constraints of a liturgical setting, there is often little or no opportunity to explain the complex history of the church's interfaith relations. Christians who remain conditioned by the lingering effects of the "teaching of contempt," and who lack any corrective knowledge, will likely interpret the proclaimed scripture in a supersessionist key.[8]

Other problem areas include the manner in which passion plays and dramatizations of the Gospels are conducted. "Bad" Jews dressed in black, selective use of religious symbols, crowd scenes with the demand that Jesus

TWELVE KEY THEMES

be crucified: the sensitivities abound where stage drama is concerned, making formation and catechesis essential.[9] As one kind of response, some bishops' conferences have issued guidelines for passion plays as well as advice that discourages their communities from holding "Christianized" Passover seders during Holy Week.[10] This is where the persistent efforts of educators, preachers, and formators working together through a variety of forums can exert a healing influence over time. Addressing supersessionism, including its "softer" and more subtle forms, remains an ongoing challenge for Catholic religious education and clergy formation today.

CHECKLIST FOR TEACHERS AND HOMILISTS

In my teaching or preaching about the New Testament:

Is it explained that Gospel texts are often colored by the circumstances that prevailed at the time of their composition? Or are gospel verses simply cited with little regard for the complex origins of these texts?

Are the historical and exegetical complexities of the passion narratives discussed? Or is the passion story treated in a facile, uncritical manner that perpetuates polemic?

Is the Roman role in the crucifixion made clear by noting that crucifixion was a Roman practice, and that the chief priest was appointed by Pilate? Or is it minimized by failing to note these historical facts?

Scripture Is to Be Interpreted without Anti-Jewish Bias

- Is guilt for the crucifixion of Jesus placed where it belongs theologically: on all humanity? Or are students and parishioners left with the enduring impression that "the Jews" or "the Jewish leaders" are to blame?
- As far as possible, are students or parishioners made aware of the complexities of interpreting Pauline texts? Or do they read them uncritically, adopting views with anti-Jewish bias?
- Is St. Paul presented as a Jew, proud of his heritage? Or as simply a "Christian convert"?
- Is St. Paul presented as having empathy for his Jewish kin and wrestling with the issues affecting Jews and Gentiles of his day? Or is he depicted as a "Christian" opposed to Judaism because it supposedly prioritized legalism over faith and grace?

8
ANTISEMITISM IS THE ANTITHESIS OF THE GOSPEL

KEY POINTS

This chapter raises confronting issues about Christian antisemitism and its contributing role in the events that led to the Holocaust.

- Antisemitism is condemned by the Catholic Church. There is no place in Christian communities for words or behaviors that harm Jewish people and disrespect their traditions.
- Understanding the Holocaust (including Christian involvement in that history in ways both negative and positive) is essential learning for Christians. It should be placed in the context of the long history of Christian antagonism toward Jews.
- A key teaching of the Second Vatican Council is the rejection of the charge of collective Jewish responsibility for the death of Jesus ("the Jews killed Jesus/God"; the "deicide" charge) that was seen as a cornerstone of the "teaching of contempt."

Antisemitism Is the Antithesis of the Gospel

The continuing presence of antisemitism in the world calls for vigilance, including attention to its tendency to mutate and to its various guises.

NOTABLE ECCLESIAL TEXTS

Second Vatican Council

What happened in His passion cannot be charged against all the Jews, without distinction, then alive, nor against the Jews of today....

Furthermore, in her rejection of every persecution against any person, the Church, mindful of the patrimony she shares with the Jews and moved not by political reasons but by the Gospel's spiritual love, decries hatred, persecutions, displays of anti-Semitism, directed against Jews at any time and by anyone.

Besides, as the Church has always held and holds now, Christ underwent His passion and death freely, because of the sins of humanity and out of infinite love, in order that all may reach salvation. It is, therefore, the burden of the Church's preaching to proclaim the cross of Christ as the sign of God's all-embracing love and as the fountain from which every grace flows.

NA 4

French Catholic Bishops' Committee for Relations with Jews

It is a theological, historical, and juridical error to hold the Jewish people without distinction guilty of the Passion and Death of Jesus Christ.

TWELVE KEY THEMES

The Catechism of the Council of Trent already rejected this error (para 1, cap 5,11)....Contrary to what an ancient but contested catechesis has sustained, we must not deduce from the New Testament that the Jewish people were deprived of its election. Scripture as a whole asks us to recognize, on the contrary, that the fidelity of the Jewish people to the Law and Covenant is a sign of the fidelity of God toward His people.

> Statement by the French Bishops' Committee for Relations with Jews, April 16, 1973, IV b

Pontifical Commission for Religious Relations with the Jews

The fact that the Shoah took place in Europe, that is, in countries of long-standing Christian civilization, raises the question of the relation between the Nazi persecution and the attitudes down the centuries of Christians towards the Jews....

At the end of this Millennium the Catholic Church desires to express her deep sorrow for the failures of her sons and daughters in every age. This is an act of repentance (*teshuva*), since, as members of the Church, we are linked to the sins as well as the merits of all her children. The Church approaches with deep respect and great compassion the experience of extermination, the Shoah, suffered by the Jewish people during World War II. It is not a matter of mere words, but indeed of binding commitment.

> "We Remember: A Reflection on the Shoah," March 16, 1998, II, V

Antisemitism Is the Antithesis of the Gospel

Another important goal of Jewish–Catholic dialogue consists in jointly combatting all manifestations of racial discrimination against Jews and all forms of anti-Semitism, which have certainly not yet been eradicated and re-emerge in different ways in various contexts. History teaches us where even the slightest perceptible forms of anti-Semitism can lead: the human tragedy of the Shoah in which two-thirds of European Jewry were annihilated. Both faith traditions are called to maintain together an unceasing vigilance and sensitivity in the social sphere as well. Because of the strong bond of friendship between Jews and Catholics, the Catholic Church feels particularly obliged to do all that is possible with our Jewish friends to repel anti-Semitic tendencies. Pope Francis has repeatedly stressed that a Christian can never be an anti-Semite, especially because of the Jewish roots of Christianity.

"Gifts and Calling," 47

Pope John Paul II

God of our fathers,
You chose Abraham and his descendants
to bring Your Name to the nations.
We are deeply saddened by the behavior of those
who in the course of history
have caused these children of Yours to suffer,
and, asking Your forgiveness, we wish to commit
 ourselves
to genuine brotherhood
with the people of the Covenant.

Prayer at the Western Wall, Jerusalem,
March 26, 2000

TWELVE KEY THEMES

International Theological Commission

The Shoah was certainly the result of the pagan ideology that was Nazism, animated by a merciless anti-Semitism that not only despised the faith of the Jewish people, but also denied their very human dignity. Nevertheless, "it may be asked whether the Nazi persecution of the Jews was not made easier by the anti-Jewish prejudices imbedded in some Christian minds and hearts....Did Christians give every possible assistance to those being persecuted, and in particular to the persecuted Jews?" There is no doubt that there were many Christians who risked their lives to save and to help their Jewish neighbors. It seems, however, also true that "alongside such courageous men and women, the spiritual resistance and concrete action of other Christians was not that which might have been expected from Christ's followers." This fact constitutes a call to the consciences of all Christians today, so as to require "an act of repentance (*teshuva*)," and to be a stimulus to increase efforts to be "transformed by renewal of your mind" (Rom 12:2), as well as to keep a "moral and religious memory" of the injury inflicted on the Jews.

"Memory and Reconciliation: The Church and the Faults of the Past," December 1999, quoting from CRRJ, *We Remember*, 1998

Pope Benedict XVI

To remember [the Holocaust] is to do everything in our power to prevent any recurrence of such a catastrophe within the human family by building bridges of lasting friendship. It is my fervent prayer that the memory of this appalling crime will strengthen our determination to heal the wounds that for too long have sullied relations between Christians and Jews.

Address to American Jewish Delegation, Rome,
February 12, 2009

EXPLORING THE THEME

What is antisemitism? Briefly, antisemitism is hatred toward Jews. While antisemitism has ancient roots, the term itself was coined in 1879 by Wilhelm Marr, a German political activist. Antisemitism is firmly rejected in Catholic teaching, a stance that has been explicit since the Second Vatican Council. Paragraph 4 of the pioneering Declaration *Nostra Aetate* taught that the church "decries hatred, persecutions, displays of anti-Semitism, directed against Jews at any time and by anyone."

One might wonder why this repudiation of antisemitism would be hailed as a radical step in the history of the teaching of the Catholic Church. After all, shouldn't it be obvious to a church that preaches the love of Jesus Christ that every form of racism and prejudice is the antithesis of the gospel? Painful though it may be, we Catholics, along with the wider Christian world, must face up to the fact that Christianity has bought into and spread anti-Jewish sentiment for the greater part of its history. Christian rhetoric depicting the Jews as a cursed people rejected by God, supersessionary theologies, forced conversions and expulsions, the incitement of violence against Jews inspired by sermons on Jesus' passion, bizarre accusations directed at Jewish rituals, the destruction of Jewish books and of Jews

TWELVE KEY THEMES

themselves—all this is part of the history of how Christians have treated the Jewish people, in varying degrees of behavior enacted in the name of Christ.

In opening a door onto this uncomfortable subject, Christian readers are urged to begin, or to further, the process of owning and redeeming these dark chapters of Christianity's story. For, while every Jew is aware of this shadow side of Christian history, *most Catholics do not know this history*. That is why the teaching of *Nostra Aetate* is so important: it speaks out about a terrible wrong and sets the Catholic Church on a deliberate path to make things right. The Catholic Bishops of France, put it this way:

> We can pass no judgment either on the consciences of the people of that era; we are not ourselves guilty of what took place in the past; but we must be fully aware of the cost of such behavior and actions. It is our church, and we are obliged to acknowledge objectively today that ecclesiastical interests, understood in an overly restrictive sense, took priority over the demands of conscience—and we must ask ourselves why.[1]

Undoubtedly, there is profound sorrow and shame involved in acknowledging the sinful chapters of our Christian story; and at times this can seem overwhelming. However, we can also take heart knowing that we belong to a community of faith whom God loves and will never abandon, and to whom the Holy Spirit gives the courage to confess its errors and to change its ways. This entails no simple "apology;" it involves a deep, ongoing transformation of mind, heart, and actions on multiple fronts of Christian life. We can be grateful to be living in this graced moment in Christian history, however challenging the path may be. We

Antisemitism Is the Antithesis of the Gospel

can be grateful that so many among the Jewish people are prepared to give us Christians a "second chance" to make things right. We can be thankful, too, for those among our Christian ancestors who did not fail to speak out in word or action against antisemitism, who were prophets in their time, and who forged a path for us to follow. From this Christian position of humility, sorrow, and hope, let us hear and own this difficult story in the brief summary that follows.

The first "schism" in Christian history was that between the emerging communities comprised of Jewish and Gentile followers of Jesus and the mainstream Jewish communities to which Jewish disciples of Jesus originally belonged. In the early stages of the birth and maturing of a new movement within an established and ancient tradition, as Christians sought to forge an identity separate to Judaism, they came to define themselves "over and against"—rather than "with and for"—Judaism.

There is debate about whether or not, or to what extent, anti-Judaism appears in the New Testament.[2] However, there is no doubt that, by the time of the patristic era, a disturbing anti-Jewish bias emerges in the writings of the church fathers. For example, in a reflection on the crucifixion, Melito of Sardis (second century) says of the Jews, "You dashed the Lord to the ground; you, too, were dashed to the ground, and lie quite dead."[3] John Chrysostom (fourth century) described the Jews as "slayers of Christ," in whose souls "demons dwell," and who worship in "ridiculous and disgraceful synagogues" that are the shrines of those "who have been rejected, dishonored, and condemned."[4] St. Augustine (fifth century) spoke of "the unbelieving people of the Jews [who] is cursed from the earth, that is, from the Church." He developed the "witness-people" theory. Unable to explain why the Jewish people and their traditions continued to survive despite (supposedly) having lost God's

TWELVE KEY THEMES

favor, Augustine held that Jews were destined to wander the earth in exile as a sign of God's anger and judgment: "the continued preservation of the Jews will be a proof to believing Christians of the subjection merited by those who, in the pride of their kingdom, put the Lord to death."[5] Interestingly, despite these dictates from Christian authorities, there is also evidence that grassroots coexistence and fruitful exchange between followers of Jesus and mainstream Jewish communities continued in various places for a long time. Thus, we hear John Chrysostom say, "Many, I know, respect the Jews and think that their present way of life is a venerable one. This is why I hasten to uproot and tear out this deadly opinion."[6] Historical context, of course, is always an important consideration when dealing with the writings of early Christian thinkers. However, it is fair to say that eventually the culmination of supersessionist theologizing, rivalries, arguments, and dangerous tensions led to a separation into two distinct religious entities: Judaism and Christianity. This "parting of the ways" was a gradual development, occurring in different places at different times, over the first few centuries of Christian history.[7]

Sadly, the dividing line between the church and Jewish communities continued to harden as theological anti-Judaism became entwined with political power. By the fourth century, the rights of Jews were being curtailed by church and state. Notwithstanding the efforts of those, like Pope Gregory I, who held a more balanced attitude and offered some protection to Jewish communities, as time went on, anti-Judaism as a form of religious discrimination based in theological arguments developed into a more aggressive form of Christian antisemitism. This is particularly evident in church artworks of the late Middle Ages depicting Jews as blind and broken, or even as animal-like or demonic figures, in contrast to figures representing

Antisemitism Is the Antithesis of the Gospel

the regal, triumphant church. One recurring accusation arising in medieval times was the "blood libel." Jews were accused of killing and drinking the blood of a Christian child as part of their Passover rituals. As irrational and phantastic as it was, this charge of ritual murder persisted and spread, even where declared groundless by state and church authorities. As late as 1881, it was being presented as a fact of Talmudic law in a series of articles published in the well-established Catholic periodical *La Civiltà Cattolica*.[8] The "blood libel" can still be found today, operating as anti-Jewish slander.[9]

The long, entrenched history of anti-Judaism among Christians, which contradicts the very essence of Christian faith, has understandably raised the question: Was there a link between the Nazis' crimes of the twentieth century and the anti-Jewish attitudes of Christians down the centuries? While careful to distinguish between the Christian religion and the ideology of Nazism, scholarly consensus views Christian antisemitism as a contributing factor to the conditions in European society that allowed Nazism to manipulate public opinion against the Jewish population. As observed by Cardinal Walter Kasper, president of the Pontifical Council for Promoting Christian Unity (2001–10):

> Between the end of the nineteenth century and the first decades of the twentieth, even very authoritative Catholic journals published articles in an anti-Semitic vein, and "more generally fanned anti-Jewish prejudices; they stemmed from the Medieval 'teaching of contempt,' that was a source of stereotypes and popular hatred" (J. Willebrands), so that it can be said, in this regard, that such an attitude offered a favourable context for the spread of modern anti-Semitism.[10]

TWELVE KEY THEMES

We must acknowledge that Holocaust history also contains the heroic stories of those Gentile Christians and other non-Jewish people who stood against Nazism and did what they could to protect and save Jewish lives. For many, it was at the risk and cost of their own lives and those of their families. Yad Vashem, the official holocaust memorial in Israel, honors many of these "righteous Gentiles," including a remarkable Indigenous Australian, William Cooper, whose story is told at the end of this book.

After World War II, as the full extent of the crimes against Jews came to light, along with awareness of the moral failures of Christians and their leaders, churches began to seriously address the sin of antisemitism. Over the years, conferences of bishops and other Christian leadership bodies have issued statements acknowledging the culpability of Christians in the fate of six million murdered Jews, including 1.5 million Jewish children. At the Second Vatican Council (1962–65), the Catholic Church effectively dismantled its "teaching of contempt" and positively embraced a commitment to a reconciled Jewish-Christian relationship. Through the Declaration *Nostra Aetate* (1965) the council fathers rejected the centuries-old deicide charge that held the Jewish people collectively responsible for the death of Jesus, although at the time there was a certain misreporting. Some media headlines suggested that the church had "pardoned" the Jews for killing Christ. In fact, what the Catholic Church said was that the Jewish people should never have been accused of collective guilt in the first place.

The 1997 text of the French Catholic Bishops is particularly noteworthy in its willingness to confront the link between the Holocaust and centuries of Christian antagonism toward Jews. In part it reads,

Antisemitism Is the Antithesis of the Gospel

> In the judgment of historians, it is a well-proven fact that for centuries, up until Vatican Council II, an anti-Jewish tradition stamped its mark in differing ways on Christian doctrine and teaching, in theology, apologetics, preaching and in the liturgy. It was on such ground that the venomous plant of hatred for the Jews was able to flourish. Hence, the heavy inheritance we still bear in our century, with all its consequences which are so difficult to wipe out. Hence our still open wounds....
>
> Even if [church authorities] condemned anti-Semitic theologies as being pagan in origin, they did not enlighten people's minds as they ought because they failed to call into question these centuries-old ideas and attitudes. This had a soporific effect on people's consciences, reducing their capacity to resist when the full violence of national-socialist anti-Semitism rose up, the diabolical and ultimate expression of hatred of the Jews....
>
> We confess this sin. We beg God's pardon, and we call upon the Jewish people to hear our words of repentance. This act of remembering calls us to an ever keener vigilance on behalf of humankind today and in the future.[11]

Statements like this are proof that people and institutions, no matter what their past, can change for the better. Yet we must also recognize that change takes time. Deep-seated sins and wounds can linger in the collective psyche and arise in new, insidious guises. Given this history, we Christians have a particular responsibility to be alert to the scourge of antisemitism where it reappears in the world around us. This vigilance calls for acute sensitivity, clarity, and courage in the face of the inevitable societal complexities. For example, we can ask: How do we combat Islamophobia and support Muslim communities while at the same time being alert to strains of antisemitic incitement in certain subcultures in the Middle East? When does criticism of the State of Israel shift from political critique to antisemitism? As Pope Francis has said, Christians of our time are called to engage with societies in a manner that is both positive and discerning, neither hostile nor naïve. In this task, we must never compromise the lessons learned from the sinful aspects of Christian history, nor lose sight of those who have suffered grievously as a result.

CHECKLIST FOR TEACHERS AND HOMILISTS

Do class or parish discussions facilitate understanding of the history of Christian animosity toward Jews (the "teaching of contempt")? Or is this topic always avoided?

Is the Holocaust treated as part of Christian history, and in the broader context of the history of Christian animosity toward Jews (e.g., the Shoah occurred in "Christian" nations; many bystanders were Christians; some heroic rescuers were Christians)? Or is it perceived simply as Jewish history without reference to Christian involvement?

Where possible, do students and parishioners engage with Shoah literature, films, speakers, testimonies of survivors? Or is the Shoah perceived as a vague historical abstraction?

Does our school or parish have a clearly articulated policy of zero tolerance for antisemitic words and behavior? Or are some antisemitic comments tolerated (as a "joke")?

When antisemitic incidents occur in the world, is it made clear to students and parishioners that the Catholic Church condemns antisemitism in all its insidious and persistent guises? Or is there an absence of discussion of these issues? Can I presume my audience understands the meaning of the term *antisemitism*?

Are teachers and clergy aware of the non-legally binding working definition of *antisemitism* (below) adopted by the International Holocaust Remembrance Alliance (IHRA), which is widely accepted internationally?

"Antisemitism is a certain perception of Jews, which may be expressed as hatred toward Jews. Rhetorical and physical manifestations of antisemitism are directed toward Jewish or non-Jewish individuals and/or their property, toward Jewish community institutions and religious facilities."[12]

9

CHRISTIANS LEARN BEST ABOUT JUDAISM FROM JEWS

KEY POINTS

This chapter continues to explore Judaism as a present-day "living tradition" (see chapter 6) and addresses the importance of Christians being attentive to the way Jews understand and define themselves.

- The transition from the "teaching of contempt" to one of respect for Jews and Judaism is an ongoing journey: education of the mind and conversion of heart.
- Deep listening to how Jews view themselves in light of their own religious experience is essential if Christians are to relate in an authentic manner to the Jewish people and their way of life.
- Catholic teaching increasingly urges respect for Jewish exegesis of scripture, as well as for the values of Judaism that can prove enriching for Christians (cf. *EG* 249).

Christians Learn Best about Judaism from Jews

NOTABLE ECCLESIAL TEXTS

Second Vatican Council

Since the spiritual patrimony common to Christians and Jews is thus so great, this sacred synod wants to foster and recommend that mutual understanding and respect which is the fruit, above all, of biblical and theological studies as well as of fraternal dialogues.

NA 4

Pontifical Commission for Religious Relations with the Jews

Christians must therefore strive to acquire a better knowledge of the basic components of the religious tradition of Judaism; they must strive to learn by what essential traits Jews define themselves in the light of their own religious experience.

"Guidelines," Preamble

Because of the unique relations that exist between Christianity and Judaism "linked together at the very level of their identity" (John Paul II, March 6, 1982)...the Jews and Judaism should not occupy an occasional and marginal place in catechesis: their presence there is essential and should be organically integrated.

"Notes," I.2

The first goal of the dialogue is to add depth to the reciprocal knowledge of Jews and Christians. One can only learn to love what one has gradually come

TWELVE KEY THEMES

to know, and one can only know truly and profoundly what one loves. This profound knowledge is accompanied by a mutual enrichment whereby the dialogue partners become the recipients of gifts.

"Gifts and Calling," 44

Pope John Paul II

May God allow Christians and Jews really to come together, to arrive at an exchange in depth, founded on their respective identifies, but never blurring it on either side, truly searching the will of God the Revealer.

Such relations can and should contribute to a richer knowledge of our own roots, and will certainly cast light on some aspects of the Christian identity just mentioned. Our common spiritual patrimony is very large.

To assess it carefully in itself and with due awareness of the faith and religious life of the Jewish people as they are professed and practiced still today can greatly help us to understand better certain aspects of the life of the Church.

Address to Episcopal Conference Delegates and Consultors of the Pontifical Commission for Religious Relations with the Jews, March 6, 1982

Pope Francis

And it is vitally important for Christians to discover and promote the knowledge of Jewish tradition in order to more authentically understand themselves.

Christians Learn Best about Judaism from Jews

The study of the Torah is also part of this fundamental commitment [to build a future together through encounter with God's word]. That is why I want to entrust your journey of research to the words of the invocation that every Jewish believer recites daily at the end of the Amidah prayer [according to the Italian rite]: "let the doors of the Torah, of wisdom, intelligence and knowledge, of nourishment and sustenance, of life, of grace, of love and of mercy and gratitude be open before You."

Preface to La Bibbia dell'Amicizia (The Bible of Friendship: Passages of the Torah / Pentateuch commented upon by Jews and Christians), ed. Marco Cassuto Morselli and Giulio Michelin (MI, Italy: San Paolo Edizioni, 2019). Unofficial English translation accessed at Dialogika

EXPLORING THE THEME

In 1974 the Pontifical Commission for Religious Relations with the Jews issued a set of "Guidelines" to help Catholics to interpret and apply the teaching of the Second Vatican Council on the Jewish-Christian relationship, as articulated in the conciliar declaration *Nostra Aetate*. A sentence often quoted from those "Guidelines" reads,

> Christians must therefore strive to acquire a better knowledge of the basic components of the religious tradition of Judaism; they must strive to learn by what essential traits Jews define themselves in the light of their own religious experience.[1]

TWELVE KEY THEMES

The second part of this sentence is particularly notable. Not only must Christians become better informed about Judaism, but their understanding should also be informed by listening to Jews. That is, they should not presume to know about Judaism without recourse to the people who actually live, breathe, embody, and interpret Jewish life as an "inside" experience. The logic of this is obvious; however, it raises the question: Why would Christians need to be told by a Vatican directive to seek out Jewish self-understanding? If, as previous chapters have shown, the links between our religious traditions are so important for Christian faith, why might Christians be prone to ignore or overlook Jews and Jewish experience?

Let's begin with a simple numerical observation. Today, Catholicism has more than 1.34 billion adherents spread across the globe. As a whole, 2.38 billion Christians make up a third of Earth's 7.89 billion people. Contrast these figures with the less than 15 million Jews who make up 0.2 percent of the world's population. There are places in the world where many people, Catholics among them, have never met a Jew and have little or no opportunity to do so. This demographic alone is one reason why Jews and Judaism can tend to be overlooked or relegated to the periphery of Catholic education. If most Catholics, clergy and laity alike, have little or nothing to do with Jewish people on a daily basis, then "relations with Jews" can seem like a remote issue compared to any number of pressing priorities that dominate the agenda of Catholic community life.

Contrast this situation with ecclesial documents of the past several decades, including the Vatican's recently revised *Directory for Catechesis* (2020), which have repeatedly urged Catholic clergy, catechists, and teachers to make Judaism an integral part of Catholic catechesis. *Integral*, not *peripheral*, is the operative word here. A numerically

Christians Learn Best about Judaism from Jews

tiny people of less than 15 million Jews has something to offer 1.34 billion Catholics (2.38 billion Christians) that is integral to the latter's religious understanding. This is an intriguing thought, but not one that captures the imagination of many Catholics.

A deeper reason for general Catholic ignorance of Jewish experience today is that we have been conditioned by a long history of Christian anti-Judaism. A Christian superiority complex, combined with negative stereotypes of Judaism, has done untold harm to Jews. It has also impoverished Christians, feeding inadequate information and at times blatantly false accusations into channels of catechesis and homiletics. A common misconception, for example, is that Jews are a "race," or, alternatively, they are simply a "religion," or a "nation." In actual fact, Jews understand themselves to be "a people," tracing their origins to biblical times (expressed in the stories of Abraham and Sarah and their descendants). Ethnicity, religion, and nation-building are factored into their identity as a people, but none of these factors alone accurately defines "a Jew." Certainly, the religion of Judaism, Jewish kinship ties, Jewish cultural expressions, and the land of Israel are integral to Jewish peoplehood. And yet, a person can be fully a member of the Jewish people and be an atheist; Jewish, yet never have set foot in the land of Israel; Jewish with dark or light skin, formed by Eastern or Western cultures, and speaking the vernacular of whatever country they live in and call home. Such is the complexity of Jewish peoplehood, yet we are prone to miss the subtleties if we are listening to typecasts of Jews rather than to Jewish people themselves.

Other misconceptions about Jews are more disturbing. The medieval "blood libel" is one example. According to this bizarre claim, Jews were involved in murdering Christian children and using their blood in their annual

TWELVE KEY THEMES

Passover rituals. As absurd as it is, the notion of "blood libel" continues to echo in parts of the world today, exacerbated by extremist social media forums, emanating from the Right and the Left, from Western as well as Middle Eastern subcultures. Other hateful accusations still circulating today include the idea that Jews are stingy with money, untrustworthy in business, and powerfully controlling of the political, economic, or media agenda. In some quarters, "the Jewish lobby" is used as a pejorative term, as if somehow Jewish advocacy for issues of deep concern to the Jewish community automatically makes it suspect. Meanwhile, the advocacy work of other communities, including that of the Catholic Church, is considered to be the exercise of a democratic right.

Further stereotypes—more subtle and perpetuated as unintended prejudice—find their way into biblical commentary. We have noted some of these in previous chapters, such as "legalistic" Pharisees, a "vengeful" Old Testament God, and an "inclusive" Jesus who blanketly condemns an "exclusionary" Judaism. Meanwhile, biblical examples of Jews acting compassionately, lovingly, and open-mindedly go unacknowledged in their "Jewishness." Within this distorted frame of reference, Christian reflections on a loving God come at the expense of a true picture of how Jews relate to the same loving God. Little wonder, then, that in a bid to dismantle the "teaching of contempt," Vatican documents today urge Christians to understand Judaism on its own terms. What one "thinks" to be a Jewish belief or practice may not be so at all. We need to go the Jewish people and listen to how they define and understand themselves and their own beliefs, texts, practices, and traditions. There is a massive listening exercise owed to this people of the Covenant from Christian communities who for so long turned a

Christians Learn Best about Judaism from Jews

deaf ear. We can take heart that the listening has begun. It is only a beginning, but it has begun.²

What happens when we begin to pay attention to Jewish self-understanding? For one thing, we become aware of the plurality of Jewish expression today. We discover that there are Jews and Jewish communities who describe themselves as Orthodox (Modern Orthodox, Haredi), Conservative/Masorti, Reform/Progressive, Reconstructionist, and so on, not to mention broad differentiations such as Ashkenazi and Sephardic or Mizrahi cultural origins and customs. Given the diversity of Jewish life, on many issues there is no one single Jewish "profile" or Jewish position. Even questions as to what constitutes Jewish identity evokes robust debate within Jewish circles.³ Whilst Jews are an identifiable people and Judaism is an identifiable religion, the Jewish people do not have the equivalent of a pope or an episcopal college or a set of doctrines that can be summed up in an official document like the *Catechism of the Catholic Church*. Not all Jews define themselves in religious terms. Further, there is diversity of ethnic and cultural expression within Judaism and Jewish life. Many people who picture Jews predominantly in terms of European heritage would be surprised to learn, for example, that nearly half of Jews living in the State of Israel today are of Middle Eastern descent, a fact that is shaping the nature of Israeli society itself, including popular foods and music. Politically, too, even on issues such as the State of Israel, Jewish opinion traverses a wide spectrum. Robust internal debates are part and parcel of Israeli society and of Jewish community life generally. What is striking is that, amidst such an array of "difference"—with all its associated tensions—Jews have managed to stay united as an identifiable people.

In listening to and being in contact with observant Jews living their traditions and interpreting their texts, a

TWELVE KEY THEMES

Christian is often struck by how "at ease" with God Jews are in their religious experience. The awe and honor due to divine transcendence and majesty does not preclude a profound sense of the Almighty's nearness and the divine desire for human beings to be intimately close to their Creator and engaged in the work of redemption. This dynamic is evident in myriad settings, from the praise of God in synagogue worship, to the personal relationships of the home, to the care of the vulnerable in society. It carries over to Torah study. Take, for example, scripture references to ancient Jewish ritual sacrifice (a practice that ended with the destruction of the Jewish Temple in 70 CE). It is an eye-opener for a Christian who has typically thought of ancient ritual sacrifice as a rather remote, exterior, hollow way of relating to the divine, to discover Jewish commentators interpreting these same texts in terms of intense intimacy. In biblical memory the people of Israel "draw near"[4] to their God by bringing items for sacrificial offering from the agricultural produce and livestock that sustain their daily lives. This is done with all the visceral reactions of love and fidelity that Christians readily attribute to their own spiritual yearning to draw close to God in their daily lives.[5] Christian-formulated stereotypes that reduce temple ritual to empty, sterile "ritualism" miss the beauty of God's word speaking to the human heart through such texts, which Jewish interpreters so readily explore for contemporary living.[6] In today's post-*Nostra Aetate* church, Catholics are being asked to listen to Jewish experience, to Jewish self-definition, and to Judaism's interpretation of its own sacred texts.

All this raises an issue of a very practical nature. In order to understand Judaism on Jewish terms, Christians require opportunities to come in contact with Jews, their traditions and writings, their synagogues and homes. Face-to-face encounters are not always a simple matter, given the demographics mentioned above. Nor should Jewish hospitality be automatically presumed in view of the history of Christian antagonism. Yet, by and large, and certainly in this author's experience in different places and countries, Jewish communities are welcoming and hospitable. Where possible, today many wonderful encounters do occur through interfaith exchanges between school groups, places of worship, and families. Events like these are invaluable to healing the past and charting a new era in dialogue and reconciliation.

CHECKLIST FOR TEACHERS AND HOMILISTS

Have my students or parishioners ever heard the CRRJ instruction that Christians ought to learn from Jews "by what essential traits Jews define themselves in the light of their own religious experience"?[7] Or is there little or no concern to learn how Jews define and understand themselves?

Are students and parishioners given the opportunity to engage with and learn from local Jewish communities (e.g., visits to each other's places of worship, joint service projects, guest speakers, forums of dialogue)? Or do they have little opportunity or encouragement to meet and learn from Jewish people? In places where there is no Jewish population, how can we think creatively about ways to make these interfaith connections, for example, through use of videoconferencing services and virtual tours?

TWELVE KEY THEMES

Are Jewish stereotypes allowed to reign within classroom or parish discussion? Or are these appropriately challenged with appeal to sound information, including from Jewish sources?

In classroom or parish discussions, is Judaism only spoken of in one-dimensional or monolithic terms? Or is the diversity of Jewish expression acknowledged and explored?

Do lessons and homilies acknowledge the ongoing salvific role of Judaism in Jewish terms (e.g., as the "sanctification of the Name") as well as Christian terms? Or is "salvation" viewed exclusively in Christian terms?

10

JEWS AND CHRISTIANS WORK TOGETHER TO HEAL THE WORLD

KEY POINTS

This chapter invites reflection on initiatives of joint social action and service among Christians and Jews, as part of Jewish-Christian relations in our time.

- Jews and Christians share messianic hope, albeit in different ways, and work together toward a future day, known to God alone, when all peoples will serve God "shoulder to shoulder" (cf. Zeph 3:9; *NA* 4).
- The growing practice of dialogue, mutual learning, and cooperative works of service between Christians and Jews is to be encouraged; it bears witness to God.
- While the significant, unresolved credal differences between Christians and Jews continue to present challenges for Christian theology, the Catholic Church entrusts these tensions to a greater mystery in accordance with God's loving purpose for the world and its peoples.

TWELVE KEY THEMES

NOTABLE ECCLESIAL TEXTS

Second Vatican Council

In company with the Prophets and the same Apostle, the Church awaits that day, known to God alone, on which all peoples will address the Lord in a single voice and "serve him shoulder to shoulder" (Soph. 3:9).

NA 4

Pontifical Commission for Religious Relations with the Jews

Jewish and Christian tradition, grounded on the Word of God, is aware of the value of the human person, the image of God. Love of the same God must show itself in effective action for the good of humanity. In the spirit of the prophets, Jews and Christians will work willingly together, seeking social justice and peace at every level—local, national and international. At the same time, such collaboration can do much to foster mutual understanding and esteem.

"Guidelines," IV

One important goal of Jewish-Christian dialogue certainly consists in joint engagement throughout the world for justice, peace, conservation of creation, and reconciliation....

Justice and peace, however, should not simply be abstractions within dialogue, but should also be evidenced in tangible ways. The social-charitable sphere provides a rich field of activity,

Jews and Christians Work Together to Heal the World

since both Jewish and Christian ethics include the imperative to support the poor, disadvantaged and sick....

When Jews and Christians make a joint contribution through concrete humanitarian aid for justice and peace in the world, they bear witness to the loving care of God. No longer in confrontational opposition but cooperating side by side, Jews and Christians should seek to strive for a better world.

"Gifts and Calling," 46, 48, 49

Pope John Paul II

Jews and Christians, as children of Abraham, are called to be a blessing for the world...by committing themselves together for peace and justice among all men and peoples, with the fullness and depth that God himself intended us to have, and with the readiness for sacrifices that this goal may demand.

Address to Representatives of the West German Jewish Community, Mainz, November 17, 1980

Pope Francis

We [Christians and Jews] can also share many ethical convictions and a common concern for justice and the development of peoples.

EG 249

In the fight against hatred and antisemitism, an important tool is interreligious dialogue, aimed at promoting a commitment to peace, mutual respect, the protection of life, religious freedom, and the care of creation. Jews and Christians, moreover, share a rich spiritual heritage, which allows us to do much good together.

Address to the American Jewish Committee,
Rome, March 12, 2019

Jewish statement:

The Conference of European Rabbis, the Rabbinical Council of America, and the Chief Rabbinate of Israel

Despite the irreconcilable theological differences, we Jews view Catholics as our partners, close allies, friends and brothers in our mutual quest for a better world blessed with peace, social justice and security.

"Between Jerusalem and Rome: Reflections on
50 Years of Nostra Aetate," August 31, 2017

EXPLORING THE THEME

One tangible means by which Christians build positive relations with Jews (and with people of other religious traditions) is shared endeavors of social solidarity and humanitarian outreach. Catholic ecclesial documents refer to this as the "dialogue of action" undertaken "for the integral development and liberation of people."[1] For many twenty-first-century Catholics, such interreligious cooperation is taken for granted. In recent years, much good has been accomplished by joint religious advocacy for the poor, for refugees, for those at risk in human trafficking, for environmental protection, bioethical principles, and so on. It

Jews and Christians Work Together to Heal the World

is good to pause to consider the milestone this represents in interreligious relations. Religious communities, including the Catholic Church, have come a long way in moving beyond insularity and prejudice to being ready to accompany one another in the work of justice and peace.

Within all streams of Judaism today there is found an openness to engage in dialogue, although some segments of the Jewish community are more hesitant, depending upon the kind of dialogue involved. For example, the influential twentieth-century leader of Jewish Orthodoxy in the United States, Rabbi Joseph Soloveitchik (1903–93), actively discouraged dialogue in matters of faith. He believed one's relationship with God to be too private and intimate a matter for public discussion outside the parameters of one's religious community. However, he considered social action to be a permitted, legitimate, and worthy way for religious communities to come together in service of the wider human family.[2] There are segments of the Jewish community today that still hold to Soloveitchik's position, or a modified version of it. As Western societies like Australia become increasingly secularized, leaders of religious communities are more likely to seek the support of one another in political advocacy to protect certain values and ethical frameworks held in common. Thus, today Jewish and Catholic leaders often find themselves working together, even if the expressed united position is not always reflected consistently throughout the religiously observant populations of either community.

From the Catholic side, the shift toward shared social action is fuelled by both practical necessity and biblical/theological imperatives. Speaking in Mainz, West Germany, in 1980, Pope John Paul II observed that Judaism and Christianity, along with Islam, "gave the world faith in the one, ineffable God who speaks to us, and...desire to serve

TWELVE KEY THEMES

him on behalf of the whole world." Steeped in the Genesis creation accounts, Judaism and Christianity (and Islam, too, through use of these creation stories in the Quran) recognize the sovereignty of God over creation, the dignity of man and woman created in the image of God, the sanctity of human life, and the responsibility of human beings as stewards of the earth and its produce.

These scriptures are sometimes described as portraying "universal" values. Indeed, they are harvested for profound insights that can speak to the human heart, hold wide appeal, and have been adopted by whole societies. We are familiar with the claim that "Judeo-Christian values"[3] underpin some of our most admirable societal aspirations and, to a degree, achievements: respect for the conscience and rights of the individual; concern for the common good; the equality of human beings before the law; a society without class distinctions where people can prosper by their own meritorious efforts; the rejection of human degradation and slavery; society's responsibilities to its most vulnerable members. The seeds of such principles, incarnated in human social structures (albeit imperfectly), can be traced to the genius of the Hebrew Scriptures/Old Testament,[4] and are rightly claimed as foundational by both Jewish and Christian religious traditions. However, we should not lose sight of the fact that these scriptures originate in a specific religious community: that of ancient Israel. While interacting with and influenced by its surroundings and neighbors, the Israelites gradually forged an identifiable path of their own. In becoming conscious of their experience of relating to the one living God, creator of all, the people of Israel intuited the divine concern for all humankind and for the entire cosmos. In other words, a *particular* religious experience associated with these texts opens up to a *universal* horizon for Israel, which is inherited by Christianity and Islam, and which speaks to the broader human family as well.

As the Genesis narrative unfolds, we learn that God blesses Abraham in order that he and his descendants may be a blessing to the nations of the earth (Gen 12:2–3; 18:18; 26:4). The universal implication of this calling given to the single figure of Abraham is foundational for Jewish self-understanding, its ethical system and praxis. It is also foundational for the church in its vocation of service to humanity, a vocation interpreted through the lens of Jesus Christ, universal Savior. In Catholic ecclesial documents, statements about shared humanitarian values and collective witness abound, such as this one by Pope John Paul II:

> Jews and Christians, as children of Abraham, are called to be a blessing for the world [cf. Gen 12:2ff.], by committing themselves together for peace and justice among all [men and women] and peoples, with the fullness and depth that God himself intended us to have, and with the readiness for sacrifices that this goal may demand.[5]

To fully appreciate the groundbreaking significance of statements like this, it is necessary to recall the history of a particularly hateful trope depicting Jews as insular, greedy, and self-serving. In sharp contrast, today's Christians can readily acknowledge the Abrahamic blessing, with its inbuilt concern for the whole human family, as characteristic of Jewish religious thought. It is admirably embodied in innumerable expressions of Jewish life, including charitable works, innovation for the common good and human rights. Information technology, science, medicine, psychology, business, law, philosophy, literature, cinema, emergency responses to global crises—in countless areas the exertion of Jewish minds and hands, the contributions

TWELVE KEY THEMES

of Jewish individuals, families, and communities, has been nothing short of breathtaking in its creativity, scope, and impact for the common good. One does not have to look far to find philanthropic Jewish initiatives grounded in religious imperatives such as the Golden Rule[6] and in the Torah's repeated emphasis on God's concern for "the stranger, the widow, the orphan." Of course, no person or human community is perfect. Jewish communities have their failings, which their external critics, and Jews themselves, are quick to point out. Yet, on balance, it would be amiss for a chapter like this to ignore the fact that Jewish "giving" to human society is remarkable, and even disproportionate to numerical Jewish presence in the world, as borne out by the count of Nobel prize winners. Pondering this disproportion, the internationally renowned religious leader Rabbi Jonathan Sacks once pointed to a fundamental attitude shaped by Torah:

> To be a Jew is to be asked to give, to contribute, to make a difference, to help in the monumental task that has engaged Jews since the dawn of our history, to make the world a home for the Divine presence, a place of justice, compassion, human dignity, and the sanctity of life. Though our ancestors cherished their relationship with God, they never saw it as a privilege. They knew it was a responsibility.[7]

For Catholics, these words readily resonate with the gospel message and with the principles of Catholic Social Teaching.

A further theological basis for joint humanitarian action among Christians and Jews lies in perspectives on the end-times. A value that both traditions share is *hope*.

Jews and Christians Work Together to Heal the World

Christians look forward to the *parousia* when Christ will come again and salvation will be manifested in all fullness. Many religious Jews look forward to the age to come when the just and merciful ways of God will be definitively established. Meanwhile, in the journey toward that day, both Christians and Jews see themselves as servants of God's redemptive activity for a world of justice and peace. The Second Vatican Council put it this way: "The Church awaits that day, known to God alone, on which all peoples will address the Lord in a single voice and 'serve him shoulder to shoulder' (Soph. 3:9)."[8]

Just as Jews with messianic hope look to the future and actively work for the healing of a wounded world (the Hebrew term is *tikkun olam*), so are Christians called to give of themselves in the service of God's reign. In this sense, and despite significant credal differences, messianic hope can be a uniting factor for Christians and Jews. We wait together, and we work together, for the fullness of the world's redemption. In the words of Cardinal Walter Kasper, President of the Pontifical Council for Promoting Christian Unity (2001–2010):

> As Jews and Christians, we have been entrusted with an immense human, religious and ethical potential against the great destructive capacity of our world—a potential which can help to build a new civilization of life. We have therefore a common responsibility for the future....We should not only cast our glance backward to the sorrowful moments of our history; today we are called to look forward and to initiate a new common history for the good of all. This is our common challenge today.[9]

TWELVE KEY THEMES

CHECKLIST FOR TEACHERS AND HOMILISTS

Are the positive contributions of Jewish individuals and communities to the common good appropriately noted where relevant to class or parish learnings? Or are they never mentioned or pointed out?

In the social justice and humanitarian projects of my Catholic parish or school, do we ever consider inviting the cooperation of Jewish communities, where practical and appropriate? Or is this a thought that never occurs?

Are the sacred texts of the Hebrew Scriptures/Old Testament presented as the healing, redeeming word of God that continues to call both Jews and Christians to life-giving action and service in the world today? Or are they treated as a remnant of the past, useful only as a precursor to the advent of Jesus and Christianity?

Is God's promise to Abram (Abraham) in the Book of Genesis ("in you all the families of the earth shall be blessed," Gen 12:3) appreciated as having a universalist meaning in Judaism as well as in Christianity? Or is it seen as having a "Christian" universalist meaning only, while Judaism is deemed "insular"?

11

THE CATHOLIC CHURCH DOES NOT SEEK TO CONVERT JEWS

KEY POINTS

This chapter introduces the painful subject of the long history of Christian efforts to convert Jews and the change in Catholic practice that has occurred in this regard over recent decades.

- In the course of history, Christian antagonism toward Jews at times extended to forced conversions. The Catholic Church today deeply regrets these sinful actions.
- If conversion of Jews is understood as part of a "mission" to lead people away from the worship of false gods and idols, then this cannot apply to the Jewish people who are in a covenantal relationship with the one saving God. The institutional Catholic response to the Jewish people today is to seek, not converts but dialogue and reconciliation.
- In concrete terms, today "the Catholic Church neither conducts nor supports any specific

TWELVE KEY THEMES

institutional mission work directed towards Jews" ("Gifts and Calling," 40). However, many deep, complex theological questions remain that are the focus of scholarly enquiry.

NOTABLE ECCLESIAL TEXTS

Second Vatican Council

Since the spiritual patrimony common to Christians and Jews is thus so great, this sacred synod wants to foster and recommend that mutual understanding and respect which is the fruit, above all, of biblical and theological studies as well as of fraternal dialogues.

NA 4

Pope John Paul II

No one is unaware that the fundamental difference from the very beginning has been the attachment of us Catholics to the person and teaching of Jesus of Nazareth, a son of your People, from which were also born the Virgin Mary, the Apostles who were the "foundations and pillars of the Church" and the greater part of the first Christian community. But this attachment is located in the order of faith, that is to say in the free assent of the mind and heart guided by the Spirit, and it can never be the object of exterior pressure, in one sense or the other. This is the reason why we wish to deepen dialogue in loyalty and friendship, in respect for one another's intimate convictions, taking as a fundamental basis the elements of the

Revelation which we have in common, as a "great spiritual patrimony" (cf. *Nostra Aetate*, 4).

Address at the Great Synagogue of Rome,
April 13, 1986

Pope Benedict XVI

Trust is undeniably an essential element of effective dialogue. Today I have the opportunity to repeat that the Catholic Church is irrevocably committed to the path chosen at the Second Vatican Council for a genuine and lasting reconciliation between Christians and Jews. As the Declaration *Nostra Aetate* makes clear, the Church continues to value the spiritual patrimony common to Christians and Jews and desires an ever deeper mutual understanding and respect through biblical and theological studies as well as fraternal dialogues.

Greetings to the Chief Rabbis of Israel,
May 12, 2009

Pope Emeritus Benedict XVI

Jews and Christians [disagree] on the correct understanding of God's promises to Israel: Christianity exists only because after the destruction of the temple and following the life and death of Jesus of Nazareth, a community formed around Jesus that was convinced that the Hebrew Bible as a whole should be enacted and interpreted through Jesus. But this conviction was not shared by the majority of the Jewish people. Thus, the dispute originated over whether one or the other interpretation was correct. Unfortunately, this dispute has often or almost always not been conducted by Christians with due respect for the other side. Instead, the sad history of Christian anti-Judaism has unfolded, which ultimately leads to the anti-Christianity and anti-Judaism of the Nazis and stands before us with Auschwitz as its sad climax.

In the meantime, it is important that the dialogue on the correct interpretation of the Bible of the Jewish people be continued between the two communities whose faith is based on this interpretation....As far as humans can foresee, this dialogue within ongoing history will never lead to an agreement between the two interpretations: this is God's business at the end of history. For now it remains to both sides to struggle for the proper insight and to reverentially respect the perspective of the other side.

Letter to Rabbi Arie Folger, August 23, 2018

Pontifical Commission for Religious Relations with the Jews

It is easy to understand that the so-called "mission to the Jews" is a very delicate and sensitive matter for Jews because, in their eyes, it involves the very existence of the Jewish people. This question also proves to be awkward for Christians, because for them the universal salvific significance of Jesus Christ and consequently the universal mission of the Church are of fundamental importance. The Church is therefore obliged to view evangelisation to Jews, who believe in the one God, in a different manner from that to people

The Catholic Church Does Not Seek to Convert Jews

of other religions and world views. In concrete terms this means that the Catholic Church neither conducts nor supports any specific institutional mission work directed towards Jews. While there is a principled rejection of an institutional Jewish mission, Christians are nonetheless called to bear witness to their faith in Jesus Christ also to Jews, although they should do so in a humble and sensitive manner, acknowledging that Jews are bearers of God's Word, and particularly in view of the great tragedy of the Shoah....

Christians must put their trust in God, who will carry out his universal plan of salvation in ways that only he knows, for they are witnesses to Christ, but they do not themselves have to implement the salvation of humankind. Zeal for the "house of the Lord" and confident trust in the victorious deeds of God belong together.

"Gifts and Calling," 40, 42

EXPLORING THE THEME

Does the Catholic Church have a mission to convert Jews?

If by this question we have in mind a deliberate effort on the part of the church to attract converts from among Jews, and if we were to examine what the Catholic Church has *done* in this regard in an official capacity over past decades since Vatican II, then the answer would have to be a resounding no. For all practical purposes, the Catholic Church today no longer sponsors any form of ministry directed toward encouraging Jews to express faith in Jesus Christ or to join the community of the church. This

TWELVE KEY THEMES

situation was explicitly articulated in a 2015 document of the Pontifical Commission for Religious Relations with the Jews: "In concrete terms this means that the Catholic Church neither conducts nor supports any specific institutional mission work directed towards Jews."[1]

As clear as this answer may be, however, it is just the tip of the iceberg beneath which lie complex, nuanced discussions. This chapter will attempt to name some of those complexities. In doing so, we will build on points discussed in previous chapters.

To begin with, we should be aware that the subject of proselytization in Jewish-Christian dialogue is an especially delicate one, for both Jews and Christians. It touches a deep nerve in Christians because proclaiming Christ is intrinsic to the life of discipleship. Due in no small part to St. Paul, the early communities of Jesus' followers were built on a missionary premise, preaching the good news of Jesus Christ, "to the Jew first" (Rom 1:16), and to the Gentiles. Announcing Christ is part of the Christian's "spiritual DNA"; it is not an optional extra. If, then, the Catholic Church now refrains from missionary activity toward the Jewish people, how is this to be explained in light of the obligation on Christian disciples to proclaim the name of Jesus Christ and "make disciples of all nations" (Matt 28:19; cf. Luke 24:47)? Understandably, some Catholics are uneasy about this ecclesial development and question its basis.[2]

Yet the issue is even more sensitive from the Jewish side. For mainstream (i.e., nearly all) Jews, any talk of a Christian "mission" toward their people is regarded as a matter with existential, and not only religious, consequences; it is seen as impacting the very survival of the Jewish people. The dark history of Christian anti-Jewish prejudice (see chapter 8)—with its efforts to suppress Jewish religious

The Catholic Church Does Not Seek to Convert Jews

practice, including forced conversions and expulsions, all of which foreshadowed the near annihilation of Jews in the Holocaust—is the terrible backdrop to the subject of Christian "mission." Many Christians were complicit in events that ultimately led to the Nazi-driven plan to rid the world of Jews. What, then, does it say for Christians to now employ proselytizing methods to "absorb" Jews into the church, thereby effectively eliminating identifiable Jewish religious practice and traditions? Is this not a form of cultural-religious genocide? The pain associated with this issue is deep and its discussion extremely neuralgic.

The cessation of a Catholic institutional mission to baptize the Jewish people, however, reflects more than a Catholic "sensitivity" to Jewish concerns—as important as this is. The Catholic Church intuits that there are deep theological reasons to cease such conversionary practices, reasons that we have already met in earlier chapters of this book.

First, if *mission* is defined as inviting people of non-Christian religions into a relationship with the living God, and awakening people to the God who loves them with an unfailing, steadfast love, then the invitation makes no sense for the Jewish people who are *already* in relationship with that same living God (see chapters 1, 3), who *already* know in the most exquisite and profound sense this God whose faithfulness endures forever—for it is the core theme that permeates the entire Hebrew Bible. In Catholic terms we can say, in the words of Cardinal Walter Kasper, who served as president of the Pontifical Commission for Religious Relations with the Jews from 2001 to 2010, "God's grace, which is the grace of Jesus Christ according to our faith, is available to all. Therefore, the Church believes that Judaism, i.e. the faithful response of the Jewish people to God's irrevocable covenant, is salvific for them, because God is faithful to his promises."³ By refraining from a conversionary mission to Jews, the church can be viewed as honoring and witnessing to God's saving, irrevocable fidelity to Israel, a fidelity upon which the credibility of all subsequent divine promises depends.

Second, if mission is understood to involve proclamation of the word of God, then the word of God continues to be present in the world today through the diverse, time-honored Torah traditions of the Jewish people (see chapters 4, 5). It is true, of course, that there is a major difference between the distinctive Jewish witness and the Christian proclamation of the gospel, in that the latter holds that the eternal *Logos* became flesh in Jesus, who is recognized as the Messiah and universal Savior. However, this does not mean that Christian proclamation must reject or demote Judaism because of the different ways Jews and Christians engage with the grace of God's word. Popes John Paul II, Benedict XVI, and Francis are unanimous in urging ever-deepening dialogues "in loyalty and friendship, in respect for one another's intimate convictions," as Pope John Paul II put it.⁴ Indeed, Catholic ecclesial statements today respond to the Jewish no by respectfully holding it in creative tension with a profound shared yes to the one living God whose Word guides both Jews and Christians in their respective journeys.

Third, in all these aspects of conversion to the Creator and Redeemer God, the Catholic Church today affirms that the Jewish people, in their own particular way, witness to what it means to live in "right relationship" with God (i.e., in a "saving" relationship); and that this Jewish life of covenanting with God occurs alongside the witness of the church. This does not mean that there are two separate, parallel covenants—one for Jews, one for Christians (see chapter 3). Rather, the emerging theological consensus and firm direction of Catholic teaching favors the

The Catholic Church Does Not Seek to Convert Jews

conviction that Jewish and Christian covenanting present two distinctive, but related, expressions within one great covenantal movement. How to precisely articulate this relationship theologically is an ongoing question and the focus of scholarly investigations. What is becoming clearer, however, is the realization that Christian witness to the living God finds indispensable partnership in the particular living witness of mainstream Jewish communities to that same God. It is a cooperative relationship with its ancient roots,[5] to be valued, nurtured, studied, and prayerfully pondered into the future. For the church to be actively trying to wean Jews away from this blessed Jewish form of witness in order to be absorbed into Christianity, then, is not only horribly insensitive to Jews, it also undermines deep theological principles that anchor both Jewish and Christian traditions.

Still, unsettling and unresolved questions remain. Whilst the Jewish people are in covenant with God, they do not share Christianity's core convictions concerning God as Trinity and the divinity of Jesus Christ. Does that, ask some scholars, make their covenant (while deemed valid) in some way lacking or inferior to the new covenant? To say no would appear to negate core Christian doctrine (the good news of Jesus Christ is salvation for *all* peoples); while to say yes would suggest that God's original covenant-making with the Jewish people is in some way lacking, or that God has withdrawn (at least some) divine support for it. We can appreciate the theological quandary! As one Jewish scholar points out, to Jewish ears the Catholic Church can be heard as saying: the Jewish covenant is "good" and to be respected, but the Christian covenant is "better" and therefore it is desirable that Jews (voluntarily) choose to be baptized and become Christians.[6]

The problem is further compounded by the fact that, while there is no structured programmatic attempt by the

TWELVE KEY THEMES

Catholic Church to seek Jewish converts, Catholic teaching has never explicitly disavowed "mission to the Jews" per se. For some scholars, this begs the question: Is it legitimate for Christians to harbour a *desire* for Jewish conversion and to hold out an *implicit* invitation to Jews? They point out the ambiguity of Catholic responses to the question. For example, while the CRRJ document quoted above clearly affirms the validity of Jewish covenantal life and states that the Catholic Church does not support any organized mission to Jews, it also makes statements like this:

> While there is a principled rejection of an institutional Jewish mission, Christians are nonetheless called to bear witness to their faith in Jesus Christ also to Jews, although they should do so in a humble and sensitive manner, acknowledging that Jews are bearers of God's Word, and particularly in view of the great tragedy of the Shoah.[7]

Does this mean that Catholics ought to be seeking opportunities to propose faith in Christ to Jews, so long as they do it in a private capacity and in a respectful, sensitive manner?[8] While few leaders and scholars within the Catholic Church would publicly endorse this interpretation today, the presence of such ambiguity understandably raises disturbing questions. Thus, "mission" remains a potential lightning rod in Jewish-Christian dialogue. The theological discussions are deep, complex, and ongoing.

Part of the problem lies in fluid use of terminology. What exactly do we mean by *mission*, as well as related terms such as *evangelization, witness, conversion, salvation*? Clarification is especially important in view of the wide variety of Christian denominations. For example, it has been noted that Catholics often use the term *evangelization*

The Catholic Church Does Not Seek to Convert Jews

to refer to a range of activities (including prayer and justice work) focused on strengthening the church's general witness to God's love in the world and without any specific conversionary targets in mind. Meanwhile, at the other end of the spectrum, there exist particular groups of Christians who actively (and in some cases aggressively) seek converts by targeting mainstream Jewish communities; they interpret these terms very differently to the Catholic Church.[9]

Historical critical approaches to scripture (see chapter 5) are highly relevant to the issue of mission. For example, the Great Commissioning of the Gospel of Matthew, "Go therefore and make disciples of all nations" (Matt 28:19), read in historical context, can be understood as a commissioning to go to "*all the Gentiles*," since for first-century Jews, "the nations" meant the non-Jewish populations. Without attention to this historical context, our twenty-first-century ears might hear the Great Commissioning as condoning a blanket missionary approach toward every non-Christian indiscriminately. Overlooked is God's enduring covenant with the Jewish people (see chapter 3).

Another example of the importance of a historical lens relates to those texts in which St. Paul expresses an urgency in desiring his fellow Jews to embrace Christ. These Pauline texts reflect a particular first-century view that the end-times were imminent—very different to our situation today where Judaism and Christianity exist as two distinct religious entities and we entrust our participation in the end-times to the unknowable ways and timing of God.

Inevitably, many of these questions come back to our understanding of "fulfillment"—that is, what exactly does Catholic teaching mean when it says that while Jesus Christ doesn't *replace* the Old Covenant, he *fulfills* it. Certainly, *fulfillment* is a term 'hardwired' in the Christian mindset. It drives much of the discussion about the meaning of the

TWELVE KEY THEMES

new covenant. Yet fulfillment is also a complex and debated concept. It cannot be reduced to a simplistic idea of "Old Testament prophecies come true" (many haven't). It must take into account the ultimate horizon toward which all history flows. A Catholic theological view of revelation presumes a *gradual* unfolding or disclosure of God's saving activity in history (see chapters 3, 5, 7). Thus, a significant reflection of the Pontifical Biblical Commission affirms that "Jewish messianic expectation is not in vain," while also observing that "the One who is to come will have the traits of the Jesus who has already come and is already present and active among us."[10] In other words, Jews and Christians alike will find the complete fulfillment of all of God's promises to them at the end of days.

This farseeing view of revelation allows mission to be viewed as a cosmic goal, brought about by God's saving embrace of all creation at the end of time, rather than as a church-engineered strategy aimed at Jews in the present. It is devoid of any sense of *coercion* (which was rejected by Vatican II's teaching on religious freedom). Importantly, the farseeing view allows space for a distinctive Jewish witness to the word of God, as the reign of God in history unfurls.

Humility is an essential attitude in these discussions. The church today is cognizant of the reality of sin in Christian communities and calls for humble confidence, not arrogance or triumphalism, in its expression of faith. It is aware of the folly of judging others for their "unbelief" in Christ; for there are numerous factors that can account for this, from poor Christian example to the mysterious windings of the path by which God leads a person or a people. The Dogmatic Constitution on the Church (Vatican II) reminds the Christian faithful that "their exalted status is to be attributed not to their own merits but to the special grace of Christ" (*LG* 14). This same document exhorts the faithful

The Catholic Church Does Not Seek to Convert Jews

to recall the exalted status of the Jewish people to whom Christians are related, "the people to whom the testament and the promises were given and from whom Christ was born according to the flesh" (*LG* 16). The historic footage of Pope John Paul II at the Western Wall in Jerusalem in the year 2000—where he prayed a prayer of repentance for the sins of Christians against Jews—provides a fitting image for the proper context for Christian mission today.[11] All conversion, mission, and evangelization begin with the conversion of our own Christian hearts. Through Pope John Paul II's papal "body language" the Catholic Church can be heard as saying, *This* is what our mission looks like at this time in history with respect to Judaism: self-awareness, sorrow, repentance, reparation, as well as recognition and renewal, that affirms and reconciles, rather than negates and alienates, our Jewish brothers and sisters.

In short, dialogue, not conversion, characterizes the stance of the institutional church today, summed up by this statement of Pope John Paul II early in his long pontificate: "We recognize with utmost clarity that the path along which we should proceed with the Jewish religious community is one of fraternal dialogue and fruitful collaboration."[12] Thus, Catholics are guided to direct their focus on developing a deeper understanding of Jewish covenantal life; and to do so precisely by engaging with, listening to, and learning from Jews. It is a dialogue that precludes any "hidden" intention for conversion, for this would undermine the very authenticity and effectiveness of dialogue. Catholic teachers and pastoral leaders who involve their students and parishioners in educational and other mutually enriching activities with Jewish communities are living examples of the Catholic Church's orientation toward dialogue with respect to Jewish-Christian relations in our time.

TWELVE KEY THEMES

CHECKLIST FOR TEACHERS AND HOMILISTS

In presentations of church history, are students or parishioners made aware of Christian mistreatment of Jews in various historical periods, including aggressive proselytization and religious coercion? Or is persecution of Jews ignored and culpability of Christians minimized?

Do presentations of "witness" and "evangelization" ever affirm the particular witness of Jewish covenanting with God and its ongoing importance to the world? Or are these terms used as if the church is the only real "light" to the nations?

Are presentations of the church's vocation to share the good news conveyed with an attitude of humility in light of Christian shortcomings and with sensitivity toward the "other"? Or do listeners hear triumphalism and condescending one-upmanship?

Are students and parishioners invited to reflect upon the iconic image and footage of Pope John Paul II praying at the Western Wall in Jerusalem in 2000? Or are they ignorant of this historic, transformative moment in Catholic-Jewish relations?

In presentations of the "missionary" vocation of Christians, is the specific sensitivity of the term *mission* for Jewish-Christian relations ever introduced for deeper learning (e.g., are participants aware of the relevant text in CRRJ, "Gifts and Calling," 40)? Or does a nuanced discussion of mission never arise? Are students/parishioners educated in how the term *mission* in general Christian usage can be heard as having ambiguous and harmful "conversionary" connotations for Jewish listeners, and thus impede the Jewish-Christian relationship?

12

THE LAND IS INTEGRAL TO JEWISH EXPERIENCE

KEY POINTS

This chapter explores the deep, enduring connection of the Jewish people with the Land of Israel, and how the church has responded to this People-Land relationship over time.

- Even when exiled from their ancestral Land, Jews have always maintained a longing to return, to be "next year in Jerusalem," expressed in their prayer, sacred texts, and personal aspirations.
- For centuries, a dominant Christian response to the biblical Land tradition in Jewish self-consciousness was to dismiss it as obsolete and to "spiritualize" the Land. Today, however, Catholic teaching seeks to respect Jewish self-definition and Catholic scholars ponder anew the theological significance of the Land.
- In 1993 the Holy See established diplomatic relations with the State of Israel. While dedicated to a politically neutral posture in regional conflicts, the Catholic Church promotes the human rights of all who live in the Land of

The Land Is Integral to Jewish Experience

Israel/Palestine—Jews, Christians, Muslims, and all who call the Land home.

NOTABLE ECCLESIAL TEXTS

Pope Paul VI

Next to the "history of salvation," there is a "geography of salvation." Therefore, the holy places have the high honor of offering an authentic irrefragable support, enabling the Christian to come into direct contact with the environment in which "the Word became flesh and dwelt among us."

Nobis in Animo, March 25, 1974,
https://www.vatican.va/content/paul-vi/it
/apost_exhortations/documents/hf_p-vi_exh_
19740325_nobis-in-animo.html

Pope John Paul II

God is equally present in every corner of the earth, so that the whole world may be considered the "temple" of his presence.

Yet this does not take away from the fact that, just as time can be marked by *kairoi*, by special moments of grace, space too may by analogy bear the stamp of particular saving actions of God....

In relation to this common religious tendency, the Bible offers its own specific message, setting the theme of "sacred space" within the context of the history of salvation.

Letter, "Pilgrimage to Places Linked to the History of Salvation," June 29, 1999

TWELVE KEY THEMES

Pontifical Commission for Religious Relations with the Jews

The history of Israel did not end in 70 A.D. (cf. "Guidelines," II). It continued, especially in a numerous Diaspora which allowed Israel to carry to the whole world a witness—often heroic—of its fidelity to the one God and to "exalt Him in the presence of all the living" (Tobit 13:4), while preserving the memory of the land of their forefathers at the heart of their hope (Passover *Seder*). Christians are invited to understand this religious attachment which finds its roots in Biblical tradition, without however making their own any particular religious interpretation of this relationship.

...The existence of the State of Israel and its political options should be envisaged not in a perspective which is in itself religious, but in their reference to the common principles of international law. The permanence of Israel (while so many ancient peoples have disappeared without trace) is a historic fact and a sign to be interpreted within God's design. We must in any case rid ourselves of the traditional idea of a people *punished*, preserved as a living argument for Christian apologetic. It remains a chosen people, "the pure olive on which were grafted the branches of the wild olive which are the gentiles" (John Paul II, 6 March 1982, alluding to Rom 11:17-24).

"Notes," VI.25

Pontifical Biblical Commission

According to Gen 15, the Lord makes a promise to Abraham expressed in these terms: "To your

The Land Is Integral to Jewish Experience

descendants I give this land" (15:18)....The notion of promise in Gen 15 is also found in Gen 17 joined to a commandment. God imposes a general obligation of moral perfection on Abraham (17:1) and one particular positive prescription, circumcision (17:10–14). The words: "Walk before me and be blameless" (17:1) connote a total and unconditional dependence on God. The promise of a *berît* follows (17:2) and includes promises of extraordinary fecundity (17:4–6) and the gift of the land (17:8). These promises are unconditional and differ from those of the Sinai covenant (Ex 19:5–6). The word *berît* appears seventeen times in this chapter, with a basic meaning of solemn promise, but envisaging something more than a promise: here an everlasting bond is created between God and Abraham together with his posterity: "I will be your God" (Gen 17:8).

> "The Jewish People and Their Sacred Scriptures in the Christian Bible," May 24, 2001, 37

Pope Emeritus Benedict XVI

The State of Israel as such cannot be theologically classified as the fulfillment of the land promise, but is in itself a secular state, which certainly has religious bases. For the fathers of the State of Israel—Ben Gurion, Golda Meir, etc.—it was quite clear that the state they created had to be a secular state—simply because it was the only way to survive. I believe that the development of the idea of a secular state is substantially indebted to Jewish thought, according to which secularism does not mean being anti-religious. The Holy See

TWELVE KEY THEMES

was only able to establish diplomatic relations with the State of Israel on such terms. And the dispute with the Arabs and the search for peaceful coexistence with them are also bound to this view. It is not difficult, I believe, to see that in the creation of the State of Israel the fidelity of God to Israel is revealed in a mysterious way.

Letter to Rabbi Arie Folger,
August 23, 2018

Pope Francis

In union with all men and women of good will, I implore those in positions of responsibility to leave no stone unturned in the search for equitable solutions to complex problems, so that Israelis and Palestinians may live in peace. The path of dialogue, reconciliation and peace must constantly be taken up anew, courageously and tirelessly. There is simply no other way. And so I renew the appeal made in this place by Pope Benedict XVI: the right of the State of Israel to exist and to flourish in peace and security within internationally recognized borders must be universally recognized. At the same time, there must also be a recognition of the right of the Palestinian people to a sovereign homeland and their right to live with dignity and with freedom of movement. The "Two State Solution" must become reality and not remain merely a dream.

Papal visit to the Holy Land, Welcoming Address,
May 26, 2014

The Land Is Integral to Jewish Experience

Patriarch Pierbattista Pizzaballa, OFM, Latin Patriarch of Jerusalem

Jerusalem is not an easy city. She is a mother who educates and makes her children grow, like a demanding schoolteacher. The city invites us to go beyond "nice" ideas and cheap words. Ours is an incarnate faith, our Jesus is a human being, who was born here in a specific historical moment, lived, called his friends to share his own life, laughed and cried, walked paths and roads. If one forgets the Incarnation, one does not enter the soul of this city. If one idealizes it, one ends up being scandalized by it.

> "Jerusalem: Locus of the Soul," reflections published online, March 16, 2021, at the Latin Patriarchate of Jerusalem website, https://www.medialpj.org/latin-patriarch/jerusalem-locus-of-the-soul-a-mother-who-educates-and-makes-us-grow.html

EXPLORING THE THEME

A book on Catholic-Jewish relations would be incomplete without a discussion of the Jewish relationship with "the Land." Here we recall the 1974 "Guidelines" of the CRRJ, which states,

> Christians must therefore strive to acquire a better knowledge of the basic components of the religious tradition of Judaism; they must strive to learn by what essential traits Jews define themselves in the light of their own religious experience.[1]

TWELVE KEY THEMES

One of the "essential traits" by which Jews have traditionally defined themselves is an inherent sense of belonging to the Land of Israel. A longing to return to Jewish ancestral land, in the face of expulsion and exile, has found expression in the sacred texts, worship, and personal aspirations of Jews over millennia. To this day, the service of Yom Kippur ("Day of Atonement"), the most solemn day in the Jewish liturgical calendar, closes with the expressed hope, "Next year in Jerusalem." Even the seasons and soil of the physical land of Israel are implicated in Jewish prayer, as Jews throughout the world recite prayers for rain on the festival of Shavuot and seek the blessing of morning dew on Passover. If Christians are to engage Jews in dialogue, then, they cannot avoid engagement with the unity of Faith-Land-People at the core of Jewish existence.

At the outset of this discussion, we must also acknowledge the sensitivity of the topic at hand. The land of Israel/Palestine is embroiled in modern-day geopolitical disputes that fill the headlines and are hotly debated in social media feeds. Just the title of this chapter is likely to arouse strong reactions! An entanglement of issues underlies such reactions. We can name, for example, the long and complicated history of the Land, with its numerous wars and changing administrations. We can name, too, the complexity of claims and judgments applied to the Land (e.g., "promised" land, "holy" land, "disputed" land, "homeland"), each invoking certain theological or political assumptions along with their accompanying terminology (e.g., "covenant," "prophecy," "fulfillment," "justice," "self-determination," "international law"). Add to the mix the experience of belonging (to a family, a people, a nation, a cause, a political alliance), the motivations arising from ideological commitments, the will to survive, and the fear of existential threat. Little wonder our subject matter is so charged with tension.

The Land Is Integral to Jewish Experience

The task of this chapter, however, is limited. It asks, How does the Catholic Church, in light of its newfound commitment to Christian-Jewish reconciliation, respond to Jewish self-definition in relation to the Land? What does the church say (and do) in this regard? What questions are being asked? What issues are at stake?

Before proceeding further, a definition is in order. What do we mean by "the Land," and why is it "holy"? Here, "the Land" refers to that tiny strip of earth on the eastern edge of the Mediterranean Sea, at the crossroads of ancient empires and today considered "holy" by the three monotheistic world religions (Judaism, Christianity, and Islam). This Land is holy for Jews, whose ancestors have inhabited the area since ancient times, predating Christianity by more than a millennium. For religious Jews it is the land of the Bible—home of the patriarchs, matriarchs, and prophets, God's gift to the people of Israel and integral to God's ongoing fidelity to the covenant. It includes *HaKotel*, the Western Wall, in Jerusalem—the remains of the foundation of the temple, Judaism's most sacred site. Even for secular Jews who have come to the Land seeking national self-determination and a safe haven from antisemitism rather than for religious reasons, the biblical landmarks can signal a sense of belonging to a people and to a place.

The Land is holy for Christians, who have lived in the Middle East since apostolic times. It is revered for its biblical meaning, especially as the place where Jesus lived, died, and rose to life. In Jerusalem, the Church of the Holy Sepulcher (or the "Church of the Resurrection," "Church of the Anastasis") is considered the prime Christian site for veneration by Catholics and Eastern Orthodox Christians. The Land is holy, too, for Islam. That which Jews call the "Temple Mount," Muslims call "*Haram al-Sharif*" (the Noble Sanctuary). On this site stands the shrine known

TWELVE KEY THEMES

as the Dome of the Rock, commemorating the visions and the ascension of the prophet Muhammed. This, along with nearby Al-Aqsa Mosque, makes Jerusalem Islam's third holiest city, after Mecca and Medina.

You will notice that we have not defined the geographic boundaries of the Holy Land. In fact, its borders are not clear, and the biblical evidence is inconsistent. Further, the borders created by populations and nation-states intersect the area, and over time have changed. This raises an important distinction: on the one hand, there exists the "Holy Land" as a sacred place, albeit not precisely defined geographically; and on the other, there exist modern nation-states and territories with political and legal borders (whether recognized, disputed, or shifting). What we call the "Holy Land" overlaps these nation-states and territories but cannot be wholly equated with any single one of them. Further, the religious and political realms, while not unconnected, each have a distinct mode of operating that must be respected and not confused. Only a fundamentalist religious view (held by a minority of Jews and some Christians) would uncritically collapse present-day geopolitical events into ancient biblical texts.

So, given this complexity, what does the Catholic Church say about the Land? As a starting point, we can observe that Christianity has never awarded the Holy Land the same stature as is found in Judaism.[2] In Christianity, the Holy Land is of immense significance; in Judaism it is indispensable. To Christians, the Land is a holy place to visit, to venerate; and for Christians who live there, it is home. In Judaism, the Land is "home" to every Jew, and Judaism is inconceivable without the desire to foster in each new generation of Jews a love for *Eretz Yisrael*. This is not the case for Christian discipleship, which does not require such an attachment to the Land. In Christian liturgy, the "heavenly

The Land Is Integral to Jewish Experience

Jerusalem" refers to one's eternal home. Meanwhile, the Jewish liturgy speaks of a physical return to Zion, as well as a spiritual vision.

An important caveat is in order. We have observed that the Land does not hold the same priority in Christian life as it does in Jewish life. However, the Christian Palestinian voice presents another view. Writes Jamal Khader, rector of the Latin Patriarchal Seminary of Jerusalem,

> When the Bible talks about "water," "bread," "sowing the seed," and many other biblical expressions, we, the Christian Palestinians, know what the Bible means. Our culture is linked with the Land: farming, sowing, scarcity of water, and bread as a symbol of life. This cultural link is much more than understanding biblical texts; it tells our story and talks about our lives....Our connectedness to the Land is not theological or ideological; it is an existential one.[3]

Here, the "landed faith"[4] of Christian Palestinians resonates with aspects of Jewish experience, as well as that of Muslims and others whose daily existence is bound up with the Land.

The fact remains, however, that most Catholics struggle to comprehend how Jews—having mostly lived in the Diaspora for two thousand years—could remain so intensely bonded to this tiny area of the globe. The intensity of this bond does not mean that Jews have automatic, unrestrained legal rights that override the rights of other peoples resident in the Land; as noted above, there is a distinction to be made between the religious realm and geopolitics. However, the unique history of Jewish attachment to the Land does introduce an important element to Christian theological reflection. This is confronting for the church when one considers that, for most of its history—beginning with the first Christian usage of the term "holy land" by Justin Martyr in the second century—Christians saw their own faith claims as superseding any Jewish interpretation of the biblical land promise. By the fourth century, a view of the "Wandering Jew" had entered Christian writings that held Jewish statelessness to be a sign of divine punishment for refusing to accept Jesus.

Over time, the significance of the Land, especially Jerusalem, became increasingly spiritualized in Christian theology. Still, its earthly reality held sway in the practice of pilgrimage to Christian holy sites—sites that became the focus of the crusades in the Middle Ages. By this stage, any respect for Jewish indigenous links to the Land was generally absent in Christian thought, a view that persisted well into the twentieth century. The infamous words of Pope Pius X, in response to Theodore Herzl's request for support for the emergent Zionist movement of Diaspora Jews returning to the Land, capture the anti-Jewish religious sentiment prevalent in 1904:

> We cannot prevent the Jews from going to Jerusalem—but we could never sanction it. The soil of Jerusalem, if it was not always sacred, has been sanctified by the life of Jesus Christ. As the head of the Church I cannot tell you anything different. The Jews have not recognized our Lord, therefore we cannot recognize the Jewish people.[5]

How much has changed. Six decades after this exchange—after the horror of the Shoah, after a United Nations resolution endorsing the establishment of a "Jewish State"—with *Nostra Aetate* the Catholic Church was not only giving due recognition to the Jewish people but repu-

The Land Is Integral to Jewish Experience

diating Christian antisemitism. Even so, the Vatican continued to eye the Jewish relationship with the Land with caution, sensitive to the volatility of the Middle East and the vulnerable situation of Christian minorities. The State of Israel was a political hot potato at Vatican II, and *Nostra Aetate* deliberately avoided mention of the word *Israel*. It would take another twenty-eight years for the Holy See to establish diplomatic relations with the Jewish State in 1993. In large part, this was made possible by the decision to separate the Catholic-Jewish dialogue undertaken by the CRRJ, from the work of the Holy See's Secretariat of State. While the former wrestled with complex theological issues pertaining to the Land, the latter could get on with the pragmatic legalities of diplomatic recognition.[6]

In terms of the Catholic-Jewish theological dialogue, the Vatican's first official acknowledgment of the Jewish bond to the Land emerged in the 1985 "Notes" of the CRRJ.[7] Importantly, "Notes" acknowledges the continuing existence of the Jewish people as favorable to God and rejects anti-Jewish interpretations of Jewish exile, saying, "We must in any case rid ourselves of the traditional idea of a people *punished*, preserved as a living argument for Christian apologetic" (VI.25). "Notes" also includes mention of the State of Israel within a framework of international law, but without drawing any religious conclusions. The text is reiterated in summary form in the 2015 CRRJ document "Gifts and Calling":

> With regard to the "land of the forefathers" the [1985] document emphasizes: "Christians are invited to understand this religious attachment which finds its roots in Biblical tradition, without however making their own any particular religious interpretation of this relationship....The

TWELVE KEY THEMES

existence of the State of Israel and its political options should be envisaged not in a perspective which is in itself religious, but in their reference to the common principles of international law." The permanence of Israel is however to be perceived as an "historic fact and a sign to be interpreted within God's design" (VI, 1).[8]

Another notable document is the 2001 study of the Pontifical Biblical Commission (PBC), "The Jewish People and Their Sacred Scriptures in the Christian Bible." Its approach to the "Land" introduces an emphasis not found in the CRRJ statements quoted above. As pointed out by Adam Gregerman, the PBC clearly recognizes the biblical land promise in the Genesis text as referring to a geographical place; a place with present-day and future relevance because it is inseparable from the irrevocable covenant between God and the Jewish people. Arguably, this approach leaves open the *possibility* for Catholics to find some form of theological meaning in the reemergence of Jewish sovereignty in their ancestral land. Similar ideas are tentatively broached in statements by a committee of the French Catholic Bishops (1973) and by the Brazilian Catholic Bishops (1984). However, they are not ideas developed by the CRRJ. Beyond these statements, the Vatican has remained silent on the question of how the Jewish land tradition relates to the State of Israel, giving rise to a notable theological lacuna: the official Catholic position repeatedly acknowledges the continuing vitality of Jewish covenantal life, however, the land tradition integral to the Jewish covenant often goes unmentioned.[9]

While official Catholic statements about the Land are sparse, Catholic scholars of the Christian-Jewish dialogue are increasingly engaged in the task of formulating a theol-

The Land Is Integral to Jewish Experience

ogy of the Land, with a number of foundational principles proposed.[10] For example: As a first principle, all anti-Jewish prejudice is to be rejected at the outset. Second, Jews must be allowed to define their own religious experience. Third, universal values concerning the dignity of every human being must be upheld.

A fourth principle requires that biblical perspectives of the Land be anchored in historical-critical scholarship. Fundamentalist readings of the Bible are unacceptable to Catholic theology. Further, in keeping with this principle, the distinction between theological and political contexts should be upheld. The Catholic Church respects the role of politicians and diplomats to negotiate their differences using the tools available within their sphere of competence. The church does not adjudicate on political disputes but seeks to exert moral leadership in the service of social harmony, justice, and peace.

Beyond guiding principles like these, however, many questions remain. For example, while avoiding fundamentalist approaches, how should Christians actualize the biblical land promises in their own lives? How can they hold in creative tension both the particularity of Jewish experience and the universalist emphasis of Christianity? And how does the Catholic Church reconcile its commitment to see God at work in history with its hesitancy to attach religious significance to the Jewish return to the Land in recent history? For those churches with a sacramental self-understanding, "spiritual" interpretations of the Land can only take us so far. The interplay between the physical and the spiritual, the visible and invisible, is inbuilt to sacramental experience. If Catholics claim to encounter the God of all history in earthly realities, might Catholic sacramental theology provide a helpful lens for interpreting the Land?[11]

TWELVE KEY THEMES

The sacramental question is closely connected to broader questions about the sacramentality of all creation, and about human consciousness of belonging to "Mother Earth." Indigenous land rights, the displacement experienced by refugees, the ecological questions raised by *Laudato Si'*: concerns like these presume a role for "land," "earth," and geographic "place" in Christian reflection.[12] In a similar vein, scholars explore the place of "holy land" in religious consciousness.

Another theological lens present in discussions of the Land is that of covenant.[13] Now that the Catholic Church acknowledges the continuing vitality of Jewish covenantal life beyond the first century CE, it faces a massive "catch-up" task: two millennia of Jewish scholarship informing Jewish covenantal life that, until recently, has been largely ignored by Christians. Given that the Christian-Jewish dialogue extends beyond biblical texts, how should Christians engage with the Jewish attachment to the Land as it appears in the prayer, liturgy, commentaries, and actual life experience of Jewish communities over the past two thousand years? Do these expressions of Judaism lead Christians to think differently about their own relationship with the Land?

Finally, there is the ever-present lens of Catholic social teaching and the challenge of developing a theology of the Land that has coherence not simply as a theological abstraction, but that attends to the human, often painful, realities on the ground and the multiple relationships between communities and the Land from diverse religious, secular, and cultural perspectives. In speaking of Catholic communities who dwell in the Holy Land, John Pawlikowski makes the point that their spiritual histories have an important contribution to make to the development of any Catholic theology of belonging in the region:

The Land Is Integral to Jewish Experience

This is particularly true of the Arab Catholic community whose origins go back to ancient times. But the more recently emerging Hebrew-speaking Catholic community's views also need to find a place in this theology. This community's unique composition of Catholics of Jewish heritage and people who have come into Israel as foreign workers, but who have increasingly integrated into the Hebrew-speaking Catholic community, needs attention as well.[14]

As you can see, the church is on a steep learning curve in its newfound commitment to Jewish-Christian dialogue, and to dialogue at large. It is a journey undertaken amid world events affecting Jews in both Israel and the Diaspora, as well as the lives of their Christian and Muslim neighbors. These developments coincide with the increasing prosperity of the State of Israel and the continuing statelessness of Palestinian populations amidst the protracted stalemate of the Israeli-Palestinian conflict—a stalemate whose causes are hotly debated. Again, our subject encompasses a minefield of sensitivities. In fact, interfaith leaders have expressed strong concern that the good work of dialogue and education is increasingly being derailed by politically based discord pertaining to the conflict.[15]

Finally, a word about the "visceral" dimension of human discourse. No discussion, whether theological or political, is purely cerebral. Personal experiences and emotions impact cognition. A Palestinian Christian in the West Bank, whose only encounter with Jews has been Israeli soldiers at checkpoints, may struggle to comprehend a biblical text that speaks of the land promises to the people of Israel. Then again, an Israeli Jew who sees an official map from a Palestinian classroom depicting the entire land as belonging exclusively to Palestinians may question the worth of peace negotiations.

Yet there is another side to this equation. Personal experiences of compassionate outreach and respectful listening, across the divide of culture, religion, and politics, can arouse emotions that shape one's thoughts and actions toward life-giving solutions. Authentic human encounter is as vital to theology as it is to pastoral efforts for peace. Pastoral leaders and educators are uniquely placed to facilitate those interreligious, intercultural encounters. They can, and they do, make a positive difference in enabling dialogue about the Land.

CHECKLIST FOR TEACHERS AND HOMILISTS

> In discussing the otherwise profound writings of St. Augustine, an esteemed father of the church, are students/parishioners also helped to be aware of his flawed theory of the exiled, stateless Jew as a sign of divine punishment? Or is this unfortunate development ignored, hence rendering anti-Jewish sentiment acceptable to uninformed listeners?
>
> Do our teaching and preaching encourage people to "strive to understand this link between land and people which Jews have expressed in their writings and worship throughout two millennia as a longing for the homeland, holy Zion?"[16] Or is this link rejected outright or treated contemptuously (as in the derogatory use of the term *Zionism* found in some political discourse)?

The Land Is Integral to Jewish Experience

- In discussions relating to the intensely debated Israeli-Palestinian conflict, are reasonable efforts made to illuminate the complexity of the historical, political, cultural background to the conflict? Or is the matter treated in a simplistic, black-and-white manner?
- Is the right of national self-determination explicitly recognized of both the Jewish people and the Palestinians? Or is one group or the other denied this right?
- Are students/parishioners assisted to appreciate the nuances of Catholic responses to the Jewish land tradition from diverse standpoints: for example, spirituality, scripture, theology, history, politics, Catholic social teaching, interreligious dialogue, relational lived experience. Or is the Land treated one-dimensionally?

AFTERWORD

The time period of the Christian "teaching of contempt," broadly understood, is almost two thousand years, nearly the entire history of the church. The period of conscious, concerted efforts to reverse Christian anti-Judaism at the level of Catholic teaching covers roughly the past sixty years. A visual depiction of this would highlight the "unprecedented" time in which we live as Catholic Christians.

In those sixty years, the official Catholic response to the need for improved Jewish-Christian relations has made remarkably fast progress. The core of an almost two-thousand-year-old "teaching of contempt" has been dismantled and replaced with a fledgling "teaching of respect." Church teaching and praxis have undergone significant renewal, and new fronts of theological enquiry have been forged. This is an extraordinary achievement, which is open-ended in its development and holds immense implications for the future.

The challenge, at this moment in history, is for the rest of the church to "catch up," as it were, with all that has occurred. Unusually, the transformation in Jewish-Christian relations from the Catholic side has largely been led from "the top"—including Pope John XXIII, Cardinal Bea, the drafters of *Nostra Aetate*, the role of the North American bishops, the work of curial commissions, the legacy of Pope John Paul II, continuing with Popes Benedict XVI and Francis, as well as the work of scholars engaged in the theological dialogue. This is not the usual way church

Afterword

reform occurs. Typically, the grassroots church is brimming with change, while the magisterium plays "catch up." In this case, the dynamics are reversed.

The goal of this book has been to assist that "catch up" at the grassroots. It has traversed a range of themes found in the Catholic-Jewish dialogue, in a summary form. My hope is that it has offered a teacher or homilist enough insight to begin (or to further) their own journey of learning, discovery, and active involvement in the revolution that is occurring within the church of our time: the "rediscovery" of Judaism—as a religious tradition in its own right and in its profound relevance for Christian identity—and the task of reconciling with the Jewish people, giving serious credence to their irrevocable covenantal life with God.

As noted in the opening pages of this book, the path involves steps both bold and tentative: bold, because we must have the courage to go forward as the Holy Spirit leads, yet tentative in the recognition that the Catholic Church's lived expression of *Nostra Aetate* is still in its infancy. The course of the church is dependent on a great deal of new learning and careful discernment. This includes listening to what Jews are actually saying to us today in dialogue and through their living story and traditions and engagement with society. It requires us to be cognizant of the wide range of Jewish experiences, along with an equally wide range of reactions to the meaning that Christians give to Judaism. Add to this the broader context of dialogue with Islam and other religions, not to mention the "search for meaning" beyond organized religion. Such are the challenges of living in a pluralistic and complex world!

A book like this can only ever be an introductory invitation for Catholics to enter the path of learning and conversation. As Cardinal Walter Kasper and others remind us:

the task ahead is immense, and "*Nostra aetate* was only the beginning of a new beginning."[1]

On this journey of transformation, may Christians and Jews walk together as friends and allies in the service of God's healing designs for all creation.

Appendix 1
JULES & LAURE ISAAC

The French Jewish historian Jules Isaac (1877–1963) is not a household name in Catholic circles, but, in the opinion of this author, he should be.[1]

Jules Isaac should be well known to Catholics, not only for the historic role he played in the story of *Nostra Aetate* in which the Catholic Church resolutely stepped out on the path of reconciliation with the Jewish people, but for the life-giving manner in which he conducted himself in critical moments of interreligious exchange.[2] Despite having suffered grievous personal loss in the events of the Holocaust—events that he knew full well were not unconnected to historical Christian anti-Judaism—Isaac somehow found the strength of character to approach the Catholic leadership, not with bitter acrimony, but with a respectful, constructive proposal to implement change.

His wife, Laure Isaac, who was murdered in the Holocaust, is an integral part of the story. She had been deeply involved in support of Jules's research and writings that uncovered the seeds of Christian antisemitism and showed them to be an aberration of authentic Christianity. This Jewish couple deserves wider recognition in the Catholic community for how they helped the church to renew itself, recalibrating its theological and moral compass in relating to Jews and Judaism. This book is dedicated to the memory of them both, with the hope that Catholic leaders and educators will share their story with those they guide and teach. A brief summary of this story follows.

In the mid-1930s Jules Isaac was a respected French Jewish scholar with a government appointment as Inspector General of Education for the whole of France. As Hitler came to power and the war intensified across Europe, he found himself stripped of his post, his published work destroyed, and forced into hiding to escape arrest by the Nazis. Tragically, there would be no escape for his wife, Laure, and their youngest son, daughter, and son-in-law. They were rounded up one day while Isaac was away from their lodgings. All but their youngest son, Jean-Claude, perished in the Nazi-driven genocide.

Against this backdrop, one could have well understood if this husband, father, and scholar had retreated into a world of bitterness and despair. Instead, marshalling his intellectual energies and a conciliatory spirit, Isaac chose to address Jewish suffering by contributing to the healing and reform of the church. Why the church? Through experience and study, he had come to understand that while Nazism was not an expression or direct outgrowth of Christianity, it nonetheless utilized and manipulated anti-Jewish thought patterns that had been deeply embedded in Christian catechesis and culture for centuries.

From 1940 Isaac had begun researching the phenomenon of anti-Judaism as it appeared in Christian Bible commentaries, sermons, and catechisms. Describing it as the "teaching of contempt," he systematically demonstrated how it contradicted the fundamental tenets of Christian belief and was fed by historical errors and stereotypes of Jews that had no basis in real Judaism. Let's be clear: in his critique Isaac was not denouncing Christianity but

Appendix 1: Jules & Laure Isaac

rather its toxic distortions, and he did so forthrightly but without animosity.

After the war, Isaac's publications and interfaith networking, including meetings with Catholic officials, were influential.[3] In 1960, with preparations for the Second Vatican Council well underway, Isaac met with Pope John XXIII. There he tabled a list of eighteen points of Jewish-Christian contention and urged the formation of a subcommission in the council that would investigate the "teaching of contempt." According to a number of converging accounts, it was this meeting that moved the pope to include the Jewish-Christian relationship in the council agenda, which until this point had been absent.[4]

As events unfolded, Vatican II proved to be a decisive turning point in Jewish-Catholic relations. *Nostra Aetate*, the council's Declaration on the Relationship of the Church to Non-Christian Religions, devoted paragraph four to relations with the Jewish people. Despite its brevity, it was a powerful summons. Reaching back to a key testimony of St. Paul, the council embraced Christianity's Jewish roots and affirmed God's irrevocable love for the Jewish people (see Rom 11:28–29). It rejected the ingrained Christian tendency to lay collective blame on Jews for the death of Christ and made clear that antisemitism is the antithesis of the gospel.

Nostra Aetate officially inaugurated a process of reconciliation that was centuries overdue, arresting and reversing Christian speech and behavior patterns that had done untold harm to the Jewish people and to the credibility of Christianity itself. Among the preconciliar efforts of individuals and groups whose dedicated work in Jewish-Christian dialogue paved the way to *Nostra Aetate*, Isaac's voice made an outstanding contribution.

Isaac's wife, Laure—herself an active supporter of his work—was murdered along with millions of innocents at the

CATHOLIC-JEWISH RELATIONS

hands of Hitler's regime, and Jules himself only narrowly escaped capture. Neither lived to see *Nostra Aetate* promulgated, yet their achievements live on in the fruits and ongoing developments of Jewish-Christian reconciliation in our own time. I like to think that with every step by which we Catholics embrace the vision of *Nostra Aetate* and open ourselves to a deeper understanding of the Jewish-Christian relationship, we honor the memory of Jules Isaac—and that of Laure, whose last letter to her husband, dispatched from a transit camp en route to Auschwitz, read: "Save yourself for your work; the world is waiting for it."[5]

Appendix 2
WILLIAM COOPER

KRISTALLNACHT AND THE REMARKABLE STORY OF AN INDIGENOUS AUSTRALIAN

Each year, Jewish communities and others mark the anniversary of *Kristallnacht* ("Night of Broken Glass"), the night of November 9, 1938, when a Nazi rampage in Germany and Austria caused massive destruction of Jewish businesses and property, as well as physical assaults on Jews, arrests and deportations, and ninety deaths during the pogrom alone. In the absence of international protest, *Kristallnacht* marked a critical step in Nazi policy toward the "Final Solution."

Particularly sobering is that the anniversary of *Kristallnacht* recalls a specific moment in history *when there was still time* for people to speak up; a moment that passed all too silently. Evil triumphed because good people, including Christians, did nothing. Eyewitness accounts of the morning after *Kristallnacht* describe streets of shattered glass, razed synagogues, incinerated Torah scrolls, and grieving relatives of Jews murdered in the violent events. Yet, for most people around the world, the day after *Kristallnacht* was "business as usual," a day with enough of one's own problems to be taking notice of the plight of the Jews "over there."

Not so for William Cooper, an Aboriginal Australian, a Yorta Yorta man, in his late seventies, living in faraway Melbourne. In the context of the times, he was hardly the image of power. As an Indigenous person he was not even included in Australia's official population count. But when William Cooper woke to the news of *Kristallnacht* in November 1938, he responded by organizing a protest march. In a society where he was counted as nothing, he stood up to be counted as a man with a conscience and a will. With a group of supporters, Cooper walked to the German Consulate and attempted to deliver a petition decrying the "cruel persecution of the Jews." The petition, of course, was rejected. Yet more than seventy years later, in December 2010, his initiative was formally acknowledged at Israel's Yad Vashem Holocaust Memorial with the establishment of the Chair for the Study of Resistance during the Holocaust, as a tribute to William Cooper.

The William Cooper story has a number of fascinating angles to it, including the sheer nerve of Cooper himself. The fact of an elderly, marginalized Aboriginal man taking a stand against Hitler's powerful, murderous regime, is an arresting image; one that calls out every excuse of bystanders to antisemitic events. William Cooper's action was characteristic of the man. Drawing deeply from his life as a Yorta Yorta man, as well as from his Christian faith, he led a life of activism, campaigning for the rights of Indigenous Australians as well as others on the margins of society. He was someone who lived the life of a commitment to justice, never seeing the reforms for which he strived. Cooper died in 1941.

Each year on November 9, the remembrance of *Kristallnacht* is an opportune moment for Christians to consider

Appendix 2: William Cooper

their ongoing relationship with the Jewish people in light of the Holocaust and the antisemitic forces that paved its way. It is a moment when people of every culture and creed can join together to say "never again" to antisemitism and to every form of prejudice, bigotry, and racism. For Australians in particular, William Cooper has made it the anniversary for remembering what it means to do the right thing, whether or not it is likely to "succeed." No matter how small or powerless one may feel or how overwhelming the evil, there is always a right step to be taken.

GLOSSARY OF TERMS

Antisemitism. Hatred toward Jews.

Christian Bible/Scriptures. Those sacred texts regarded as divinely inspired and officially declared scripture by Christian churches.

Covenant. A sacred agreement and promise between two parties (especially between God and human beings) to live in harmony with one another according to certain obligations to be fulfilled by each party.

Dialogue. Between religious communities, the exchange of ideas, or shared prayer, or common activities in the service of reconciliation and right relations.

End-time (or *end of days*). The end of history as we know it, when the reign of God will be present in all its fullness, and all creation transformed and united in Christ.

Exegesis. The interpretation or drawing meaning out of a text, especially a biblical text.

Gnosticism. A collection of philosophical and religious ideas, with ancient roots, that prioritize spiritual "knowledge" and inner enlightenment over the body, history, and earthly existence.

Hebrew Bible/Scriptures (or "Jewish Scriptures"). Those sacred texts regarded as divinely inspired and officially declared scripture for Jews. These texts have also been incorporated into the Old Testament of the Christian Bible.

Holocaust. The mass murder of six million Jews in Europe at the direction of Adolph Hitler and the German Nazi party during the Second World War.

Incarnation. The Christian belief that "the Word became flesh and lived among us" (John 1:14); i.e., the transcendent God (eternal *Logos*) entered human history, revealed in a particular

CATHOLIC-JEWISH RELATIONS

first-century Jew, Jesus of Nazareth, who was truly God and truly man.

International Holocaust Remembrance Alliance (IHRA). An intergovernmental organization that addresses Holocaust-related issues in order to combat the persistent scourge of antisemitism.

Israel. This term has multiple meanings. It can refer to the biblical land; the name given to the patriarch Jacob or to one of the twelve tribes issuing from his progeny; the political nation state named Israel (either in its ancient or modern context). "Israel" is also a theological reference to the Jewish people, from their origins in history to their ultimate destiny in accord with God's design.

Jewish Bible/Scriptures. See Hebrew Bible.

Land promise. The recurring reference in the Hebrew Bible/Old Testament to God's covenant-making promise to gift a specific area of land to Abraham and his descendants.

Magisterium. For the Catholic Church, the magisterium is its official teaching office with the authority to make a discerning, definitive judgment as to what constitutes an authentic interpretation of God's word.

Sacramentality. In its widest sense, the capacity of material, created realities to mediate divine presence.

Second Temple Period. The centuries between the rebuilding of the first temple in Jerusalem (destroyed by the Babylonians in 586 BCE), and the destruction of the second temple by the Romans in 70 CE.

Second Vatican Council ("Vatican II"). The Second Ecumenical Council of the Vatican, called by Pope John XXIII and held in Rome, 1962 to 1965; a worldwide assembly of bishops with an agenda of renewal for the global Catholic Church.

Shoah. The Hebrew term (meaning "catastrophe") used to describe the events that are otherwise known as the Holocaust (see above).

Supersessionism. The (erroneous) belief that because Jesus has fulfilled the Old Testament promises, the church has replaced the people of Israel, making Judaism obsolete.

Glossary of Terms

TANAKH. The Jewish Bible. The acronym is derived from the first letter of each of the three divisions of the Jewish Bible: *Torah* (Teaching/Law: the books of the Pentateuch, Genesis to Deuteronomy), *Nevi'im* (Prophets: the prophetic literature), and *Ketuvim* (Writings: a collection of other texts including Psalms and Proverbs).

Teaching of contempt. A phrase coined in the twentieth century by French Jewish historian Jules Isaac to describe the long history of anti-Jewish sentiment expressed in Christian culture and catechesis.

Torah. Hebrew: "teaching," "instruction." Torah has narrow and expansive meanings in Judaism. It can refer to the first five books of the Bible (the Pentateuch), or the whole Jewish Bible, or the entire corpus of Jewish sacred writings including non-biblical works (e.g., Mishnah, Talmud).

Vatican II. See Second Vatican Council

NOTES

PREFACE

1. Yves Congar, *True and False Reform in the Church*, rev. ed., trans. Paul Philibert (Collegeville, MN: Liturgical Press, 2011), 304. In this work, Congar explores the foundational principles of the conservative-yet-innovative processes that constantly renew the inner spirit and the visible structures of the pilgrim church.

2. *Amitié Judéo-Chrétienne de France* was a pioneering association of Christians and Jews. The Ten Points of Seelisberg was a remarkable contribution of this early era of Jewish-Christian dialogue. Just after World War II, in the small Swiss village of Seelisberg, Jews and Christians met in the summer of 1947 to write guidelines to help Christians to renew their relationship with Judaism. Notable, too, is the shift in thinking that occurred in the 1950s for the Catholic Congregation of Sisters of Our Lady of Sion, and the parallel Congregation of brothers and priests of Sion. They anticipated and assisted the revision of the Catholic attitude toward Judaism even before *Nostra Aetate* was promulgated at the Second Vatican Council.

3. The term *Israel* has multiple meanings (refer to Glossary). Unless otherwise indicated, in this book it is used as a theological reference to the Jewish people, from their origins in history to their ultimate destiny in accord with God's design.

4. For an exploration of twelve similar or related themes by twenty-one Catholic and Protestant scholars, see Mary C. Boys, ed., *Seeing Judaism Anew: Christianity's Sacred Obligation* (Lanham, MD: Rowman & Littlefield, 2005).

CATHOLIC-JEWISH RELATIONS

HOW TO USE THIS BOOK

1. On the importance that the Jewish-Christian relationship engage with Islam and other religions, see John Pawlikowski, "The Uniqueness of the Christian-Jewish Dialogue: A Yes and a No," *Studies in Christian-Jewish Relations* 12 (2017): 1–14, https://doi.org/10.6017/scjr.v12i1.9799.

CHAPTER 1

1. John Connelly, *From Enemy to Brother: The Revolution in Catholic Teaching on the Jews 1933–1965* (Cambridge, MA: Harvard University Press, 2012), 5–6, 23, 286.

2. Jules Isaac, *The Teaching of Contempt: The Christian Roots of Anti-Semitism*, trans. Helen Weaver, 2nd ed. (New York: McGraw-Hill, 1965).

3. John Paul II, Address to Pontifical Biblical Commission, April 11, 1997.

4. John Paul II, Address to PBC, April 11, 1997.

5. *NA* 4; cf. Rom 9:5.

6. This is the christological insight of Hans Hermann Henrix in examining the teachings of Pope John Paul II. Hans Hermann Henrix, "The Son of God Became Human as a Jew: Implications of the Jewishness of Jesus for Christology," in *Christ Jesus and the Jewish People Today: New Explorations of Theological Interrelationships*, ed. Philip A. Cunningham et al. (Grand Rapids, MI: Eerdmans, 2011), 114–43, at 119–20.

7. *Summa Theologica* III, q.48, a.2, ad 3; cited in this regard by Bruce D. Marshall, "Religion and Election: Aquinas on Natural Law, Judaism, and Salvation in Christ," *Nova et Vetera* 14 (2016): 121.

8. This sentence originated in a statement of the German Bishops. Pope John Paul II made it his own in his Address to Representatives of the West German Jewish Community, Mainz, November 17, 1980.

Notes

CHAPTER 2

1. Cf. *NA* 4; CRRJ, "Guidelines," 1974; Pope John Paul II, Address at the Great Synagogue of Rome, April 13, 1986.
2. Address to Delegates of the Conference of Presidents of Major American Jewish Organizations, February 12, 2009.
3. PBC, "The Jewish People and Their Sacred Scriptures in the Christian Bible," May 24, 2001, 84.
4. For an introduction to the cycle of Jewish festivals as celebrated today, see Michael Strassfeld, *The Jewish Holidays* (New York: HarperCollins, 1985).
5. This phrase, arising in the theological reflections of Joseph Ratzinger (Pope Benedict XVI), has entered the discussions of the Catholic-Jewish dialogue, as in CRRJ, "Gifts and Calling," 26. See Joseph Ratzinger, *Jesus of Nazareth. From the Baptism in the Jordan to the Transfiguration*, trans. Adrian J. Walker (New York: Doubleday, 2007), 169.
6. Henri de Lubac, *The Motherhood of the Church*, trans. Sergia Englund (San Francisco: Ignatius Press, 1982), 15–18, 47–58.
7. Yves Congar, *True and False Reform in the Church*, rev. ed., trans. Paul Philibert (Collegeville, MN: Liturgical Press, 2011), 304.

CHAPTER 3

1. Emphasis added in the three quotations in this section.
2. See *LG* 16; *NA* 4.
3. Cardinal Walter Kasper, President of the Pontifical Commission for Religious Relations with the Jews, commenting on the document of the Congregation for the Doctrine of the Faith, *Dominus Iesus*, at the seventeenth meeting of the International Catholic-Jewish Liaison Committee, New York, May 1, 2001.
4. Pope Emeritus Benedict XVI, "Grace and Vocation without Remorse: Comments on the Treatise *De Iudaeis*," *Communio* 45 (Spring 2018): 180–81.

CATHOLIC-JEWISH RELATIONS

5. Gavin D'Costa, *Catholic Doctrines on the Jewish People after Vatican II* (New York: Oxford University Press, 2019), 20, 26.
6. *EG* 247.
7. Pope John Paul II, Address to Jewish Community Leaders, Sydney, November 26, 1986.

CHAPTER 4

1. Pontifical Biblical Commission, "The Jewish People and Their Sacred Scriptures in the Christian Bible," May 24, 2001, 84.
2. The term *TANAKH* is derived from the first letter of each of the three divisions of the Jewish Bible: *Torah* (Teaching/Law—the books of the Pentateuch, Genesis to Deuteronomy), *Nevi'im* (Prophets—the prophetic literature) and *Ketuvim* (Writings—a collection of other texts including Psalms and Proverbs).
3. While the Bible is not identical to divine revelation, it is a "conduit" of revelation by which the divine presence is encountered in the life of the community of faith. The scriptures are interpreted and actualized within a living tradition. See Gerald O'Collins, *Inspiration: Towards a Christian Interpretation of Biblical Inspiration* (New York: Oxford University Press, 2018), 87–100, at 88, 94.
4. PBC, "The Jewish People and Their Sacred Scriptures," 84.
5. *DV* 12.
6. Pontifical Council for the Promotion of New Evangelization, *Directory for Catechesis*, Libreria Editrice Vaticana, 2020, 348c.
7. Care and justice for people in these three categories are repeatedly called for in the Hebrew Scriptures, e.g., Deut 24:17, 19, 20.
8. PBC, "The Jewish People and their Sacred Scriptures," 22.
9. Joseph Ratzinger, *Jesus of Nazareth, Part Two, Holy Week: From the Entrance into Jerusalem to the Resurrection* (San Francisco: Ignatius Press, 2011), 32–35. Here, Pope Benedict XVI writes in his personal capacity as a theologian, whereas Pope Francis writes with the papal authority of an apostolic exhortation.
10. *EG* 249.
11. The sculpture was commissioned to mark the golden jubilee of *Nostra Aetate* in 2015 by the Institute for Jewish-Catholic

Notes

Relations at Saint Joseph's University in Philadelphia. Further information is available at the university's website, https://www.sju.edu/college-arts-and-sciences/ijcr/synagoga-ecclesia.The artwork lends itself to a "teachable moment" in a classroom or parish group.

12. PBC, "The Jewish People and Their Sacred Scriptures," 22; cf. preface by Cardinal Ratzinger.

CHAPTER 5

1. Pope John Paul II, Address at the Great Synagogue of Rome, April 13, 1986.

2. This view of history, of course, reflects a Christian perspective. From a Jewish view, the Jewish-Christian relationship is strictly interreligious. Cf. CRRJ, "Gifts and Calling," 15.

3. Since 1974, the Catholic Church's dialogue with the Jewish people has been undertaken through its Commission for Religious Relations with the Jews, which is distinct but very closely related to the Pontifical Council for Promoting Christian Unity.

4. In 1988 the Secretariat for Non-Christians was renamed the Pontifical Council for Interreligious Dialogue (PCID).

5. Jon Levenson unpacks this point in *Inheriting Abraham: The Legacy of the Patriarch in Judaism, Christianity and Islam* (Princeton, NJ: Princeton University Press, 2012). Says Levenson, to turn Abraham into a "religiously neutral" figure undermines the distinctiveness of each tradition's textual interpretations involving Abraham.

6. Of interest to Christian educators is Amy-Jill Levine and Marc Zvi Brettler, *The Bible with and without Jesus: How Jews and Christians Read the Same Stories Differently* (New York: HarperCollins, 2020).

7. For example, see Kevin J. Madigan and Jon D. Levenson, *Resurrection: The Power of God for Christians and Jews* (New Haven: Yale University Press, 2008).

8. Pope Francis, Address to the International Council of Christians and Jews, June 30, 2015.

CATHOLIC-JEWISH RELATIONS

CHAPTER 6

1. *NA* 4; emphasis added. In the Greek, this passage from Romans has no verb, however the conciliar translators correctly took note of the present tense of a preceding passage. See Eugene J. Fisher, "Official Roman Catholic Teaching on Jews and Judaism: Commentary and Context," in *In Our Time: The Flowering of Jewish-Catholic Dialogue*, ed. Eugene J. Fisher and Leon Klenicki (Mahwah, NJ: Paulist Press, 1990), 6.

2. The relational dimension is intensified for most Jews, for whom to be a Jew is to be (literally) born a Jew. While baptism rather than biological kinship defines Christian identity, the natural family unit is religiously central for Christian initiation in the case of Catholics and other Christians who practice infant baptism (hence we speak of "cradle Catholics").

3. Pope John Paul II, Address to Episcopal Conference Delegates and Consultors of the CRRJ, March 6, 1982; CRRJ, "Notes," June 24, 1985, I.3.

4. This point is stated from a Christian perspective. For Jews, the figure of Jesus can be both a uniting and dividing factor in their relationships with Christians.

5. For a theological enquiry on this point, see Hans Hermann Henrix, "The Son of God Became Human as a Jew: Implications of the Jewishness of Jesus for Christology," in *Christ Jesus and the Jewish People Today: New Explorations of Theological Interrelationships*, ed. Philip A. Cunningham et al. (Grand Rapids, MI: Eerdmans, 2011), 114–143, at 139–142.

6. *EG* 248.

7. CRRJ, "Guidelines," 25.

8. Pope John Paul II, Address, Mainz, November 17, 1980.

9. See CRRJ, "Gifts and Calling," 26.

10. Matthias Henze, *Mind the Gap: How the Jewish Writings between the Old and New Testament Help Us Understand Jesus* (Minneapolis: Fortress Press, 2017).

11. See, for example, the synthesis of traditional Jewish wisdom by the twentieth-century Jewish scholar Abraham Joshua Heschel, *Heavenly Torah as Refracted through the Generations*, ed. and trans. Gordon Tucker (New York: Continuum, 2007).

12. Walter Kasper, "The Theology of the Covenant as Cen-

Notes

tral Issue in the Jewish-Christian Dialogue," presented at Sacred Heart University in Fairfield, Connecticut, December 4, 2001.

CHAPTER 7

1. However, the church has traditionally held that "the way we worship" is "what we believe" (*lex orandi, lex credendi*); therefore it can be argued that in a certain sense the Church did teach supersessionism by way of the liturgy, for example, by reference to the "perfidious" Jews (i.e., "stubbornly unbelieving" Jews, and widely taken to mean "deceitful," "treacherous" Jews) that was once part of the Roman Catholic Good Friday liturgy. This phrase was removed in 1959 by Pope John XXIII.

2. Jon Levenson, "Did God Forgive Adam? An Exercise in Comparative Midrash," in *Jews and Christians: People of God*, ed. Carl E. Braaten and Robert W. Jenson (Grand Rapids, MI: Eerdmans, 2003), 151.

3. Matthew A. Tapie, *Aquinas on Israel and the Church: The Question of Supersessionism in the Theology of Thomas Aquinas* (Eugene, OR: Pickwick, 2014), 23–24.

4. This list is based, in part and in adapted form, on the work of Amy-Jill Levine, *The Misunderstood Jew: The Church and the Scandal of the Jewish Jesus* (San Francisco: Harper Collins, 2006), 124–25.

5. Paula Fredriksen, *When Christians Were Jews: The First Generation* (New Haven & London: Yale University Press, 2018), 185.

6. For an introduction to recent developments in Pauline scholarship, see Magnus Zetterholm, *Approaches to Paul: A Student's Guide to Recent Scholarship* (Minneapolis: Fortress Press, 2009).

7. For insights into these scholarly discussions, see John T. Pawlikowski, *Restating the Catholic Church's Relationship with the Jewish People: The Challenge of Super-Sessionary Theology* (New York: Edwin Mellen, 2013).

8. See Marilyn J. Salmon, *Preaching without Contempt: Overcoming Unintended Anti-Judaism* (Minneapolis: Augsburg Fortress, 2006).

9. Philip Cunningham, ed., *Pondering the Passion: What's at Stake for Christians and Jews?* (Lanham, MD: Rowman & Littlefield, 2004).

CATHOLIC-JEWISH RELATIONS

10. For example, U.S. Bishops' Committee for Ecumenical and Interreligious Affairs, National Conference of Catholic Bishops, "Criteria for the Evaluation of Dramatizations of the Passion," 1988.

CHAPTER 8

1. Catholic Bishops of France, Declaration of Repentance, September 30, 1997.
2. For insight into this discussion, see Terence L. Donaldson, *Jews and Anti-Judaism in the New Testament: Decision Points and Divergent Interpretations* (London: SPCK, 2010).
3. Melito of Sardis, "On the Pasch," II.99. Patristic quotations accessed at *Dialogika*.
4. Chrysostom, "Against Judaizing Christians," Homily I.6.3; 6.7; 3.7.
5. Augustine, *Contra Faustum*, Book XII, 11–12.
6. Chrysostom, "Against Judaizing Christians," Homily I.3.1.
7. Scholars debate the time frame for this process of separation, which may have extended to the fourth or fifth century. Some even argue that the ways have never fully parted. See Adam Becker and Annette Yoshiko Reed, eds., *The Ways that Never Parted: Jews and Christians in Late Antiquity and the Early Middle Ages* (Minneapolis: Fortress, 2007).
8. Paul O'Shea, *A Cross Too Heavy: Pope Pius XII and the Jews of Europe* (New York: Macmillan, 2011), 70.
9. At times the "blood libel" emerges unnervingly close to home, as in the gruesome images and slogans displayed on posters at an anti-Israel political protest rally held in the home city of this author.
10. Walter Kasper, "Antisemitism: A Wound to Be Healed: Reflections for the Fourth European Day of Jewish Culture," September 5, 2003.
11. Catholic Bishops of France, "Declaration of Repentance," September 30, 1997.
12. Accessed February 24, 2022, at the IHRA website, https://www.holocaustremembrance.com/resources/working-definitions-charters/working-definition-antisemitism.

Notes

CHAPTER 9

1. CRRJ, "Guidelines," Preamble.

2. As an example of progress, Christians today draw on the work of Jewish New Testament scholars who assist both Jews and Christians to better understand many New Testament texts in their historical and cultural context as Jewish literature. See Amy-Jill Levine and Marc Zvi Brettler, eds., *The Jewish Annotated New Testament*, rev. ed. (New York: Oxford University Press, 2017).

3. Acquaintance with the educational endeavors of Shalom Hartman Institute (hartman.org.il) in Israel and North America reveals numerous topics about Jewish identity passionately and fruitfully debated by Jews today.

4. *Korban*, the Hebrew word translated as "sacrifice," is derived from a root word meaning "to draw near, to bring close."

5. This is not to suggest that mainstream Jews aspire to rebuild the Jerusalem temple in our time or return to a system of temple sacrifice; the point here is that Torah texts about ritual sacrifice and temple worship can speak tenderly to the human heart.

6. For a notable example, see Jonathan Sack's introductory chapter to his commentary on the Book of Leviticus: *Leviticus: The Book of Holiness*, Covenant & Conversation, vol. 3 (Jerusalem: Koren Publishers, 2015), Kindle edition, location 131–998.

7. CRRJ, "Guidelines," Preamble.

CHAPTER 10

1. Pontifical Council for Interreligious Dialogue, "Dialogue and Proclamation: Reflections and Orientations on Interreligious Dialogue and the Proclamation of the Gospel of Jesus Christ," May 19, 1991, 42, accessed at the Vatican website, https://www.vatican.va/roman_curia/pontifical_councils/interelg/documents/rc_pc_interelg_doc_19051991_dialogue-and-proclamatio_en.html.

2. See Joseph B. Soloveitchik, "Confrontation," in *Bridges: Documents of the Christian-Jewish Dialogue*, vol. 1, ed. Franklin Sherman (Mahwah, NJ: Paulist Press, 2011), 405–18, at 416–17.

3. The term has a relatively recent history. It affirms ethical

principles found in both Jewish and Christian traditions, drawing on common sources, and is often used to emphasize a shared vision for societal goals. The term sometimes attracts the criticism that it masks the history of Christian anti-Judaism and overstates the unifying elements of Jewish and Christian traditions.

4. For a Jewish perspective on this point, see Reuven Hammer, *The Torah Revolution: Fourteen Truths that Changed the World* (Woodstock, VT: Jewish Lights, 2011).

5. Pope John Paul II, Address to Jewish Representatives, Mainz, November 17, 1980.

6. Widely shared by many religions and cultures, the "Golden Rule" is the principle of treating others as one would wish to be treated.

7. Jonathan Sacks, "The Way of Responsibility: The Jewish Future," *Ten Paths to God* curriculum, Unit 10, https://www.rabbisacks.org/curriculum-resources/ten-paths-to-god/.

8. *NA* 4, with a footnoted reference to Isa 66:23; Ps 65:4; Rom 11:11–32.

9. Walter Kasper, "The Theology of the Covenant as Central Issue in the Jewish-Christian Dialogue," presented at Sacred Heart University in Fairfield, Connecticut, December 4, 2001.

CHAPTER 11

1. CRRJ, "Gifts and Calling," 40.

2. For a scholarly example, see Gavin D'Costa, *Catholic Doctrines on the Jewish People after Vatican II* (New York: Oxford University Press, 2019), 144–87.

3. Address to International Catholic-Jewish Liaison Committee regarding the Declaration *Dominus Iesus*, New York, May 1, 2001.

4. Address at the Great Synagogue of Rome, April 13, 1986.

5. St. Paul was acutely aware of the mystery of Israel intimately entwined with the life of the Christ-centered communities; and from patristic times the one church is described as formed from Israel and the nations (*ecclesia ex circumcisione and ecclesia ex gentibus).*

6. Adam Gregerman, "Superiority without Supersessionism: Walter Kasper and The Gifts and the Calling of God Are Irre-

Notes

vocable, and God's Covenant with the Jews," *Theological Studies* 79, no. 1 (2018): 36–59, at 42.

7. "Gifts and Calling," 40.

8. Adam Gregerman elucidates the underappreciated ambiguities in Catholic writings associated with this question; see Gregerman, "The Desirability of Jewish Conversion to Christianity in Contemporary Catholic Thought," *Horizons* 45, no. 2 (October 2018): 249–86, at 269.

9. That Catholic teaching regards religious coercion as unacceptable is clearly stated in Vatican II, Declaration on Religious Freedom, *Dignitatis Humanae*, December 7, 1965.

10. PBC, "The Jewish People and Their Sacred Scriptures in the Christian Bible," May 24, 2001, 21.

11. Philip Cunningham has repeatedly drawn attention to the significance of this iconic image for theological discussion; see Philip Cunningham, *Seeking Shalom: The Journey to Right Relationship between Catholics and Jews* (Grand Rapids, MI: William B. Eerdmans), 149.

12. Pope John Paul II, Address to Representatives of Jewish Organizations, Rome, March 12, 1979.

CHAPTER 12

1. CRRJ, "Guidelines," Preamble.

2. This is reflected in the fact that the New Testament does not explicitly address the land promise of the Hebrew Bible/Old Testament.

3. Jamal Kader, "Theology of the Land: A Christian Palestinian Perspective," in *Enabling Dialogue About the Land*, ed. Philip A. Cunningham, Ruth Langer, and Jesper Svartvik (Mahwah, NJ: Paulist Press, 2020), 63–85, at 64.

4. A term employed by Protestant theologian Walter Brueggemann, cited in John T. Pawlikowski, "Toward A Theology of Belonging: A Catholic Christian Perspective," in *Enabling Dialogue*, ed. Cunningham et al, 262–281, at 275.

5. *The Complete Diaries of Theodor Herzl*, trans. Harry Zohn (New York: Herzl Press, 1960), 1601–5, accessed online at *Dialogika*.

6. Raymond Cohen, "Challenges of the Land and State of Israel for Christian Churches: The Example of the Vatican," in Cunningham et al., *Enabling Dialogue*, 191–212.

7. "Notes," June 24, 1985.

8. "Gifts and Calling," 5.

9. Adam Gregerman, "Is the Biblical Land Promise Irrevocable? Post-*Nostra Aetate* Catholic Theologies of the Jewish Covenant and the Land of Israel," *Modern Theology* 34:2 (April 2018): 137–58.

10. On these principles, see Philip Cunningham, "Toward a Catholic Theology of the Centrality of the Land," in Cunningham et al., *Enabling Dialogue*, 315–25, at 312–15.

11. Richard Lux reflects on the Land through the lens of Catholic sacramental theology in his work, *The Jewish People, the Holy Land, and the State of Israel: A Catholic View* (Mahwah, NJ: Paulist Press, 2010).

12. Michael Trainor, "Understanding Land and Its Ecological Connectedness: Implications for Christian-Jewish Dialogue," in Cunningham et al., *Enabling Dialogue*, 335–54.

13. On Jews and Christians as "co-covenanting" companions with respect to the Land, see Philip Cunningham, "Toward a Catholic Theology," 315–25.

14. Pawlikowski, "Toward a Theology of Belonging," 270. On Hebrew-speaking Catholics in Israel, see www.catholic.co.il.

15. One constructive response to this problem is *Enabling Dialogue about the Land*, ed. Philip A. Cunningham, Ruth Langer, and Jesper Svartvik (Mahwah, NJ: Paulist Press, 2020). This book is the fruit of several years of scholarly discussion initiated by a research project of the International Council of Christians and Jews (ICCJ). It includes the diverse views of sixteen contributors—Jewish, Christian, and Muslim—and offers pedagogical tools for facilitating respectful and productive interreligious discussions about the Land.

16. National Conference of Catholic Bishops (USA), "Guidelines for Catholic-Jewish Relations," November 20, 1975, https://www.ccjr.us/dialogika-resources/documents-and-statements/roman-catholic/us-conference-of-catholic-bishops/nccb1975.

Notes

AFTERWORD

1. Walter Kasper, "The Commission for Religious Relations with the Jews: A Crucial Endeavour of the Catholic Church," Address at Boston College, November 6, 2002, III.

APPENDIX I

1. For a scholarly work on Jules Isaac's life and contributions, see Norman Tobias, *Jewish Conscience of the Church: Jules Isaac and the Second Vatican Council* (Cham, Switzerland: Springer, 2017).

2. Isaac, a highly principled truth seeker, did not consider himself an observant religious Jew in the traditional sense. According to the testimony of their son Jean-Claude, when Jules and Laure married, "she and he, united by the same goal, established a household animated by this sole religion: 'faith in the divine virtue of creative realization.'" Quoted in Tobias, *Jewish Conscience*, 29–30.

3. Isaac's works on this theme include *Jésus et Israël* (1947), *Genèse de l'antisémitisme* (1956), and *L'Enseignement du Mépris* (1962), the latter of which was written at the age of eighty-five and published in English as *The Teaching of Contempt* (New York: McGraw-Hill, 1964).

4. Tobias, *Jewish Conscience*, 249–51.

5. Quoted by Claire Huchet Bishop in her biographic introduction to Jules Isaac, *The Teaching of Contempt*, 9. Cf. Tobias, *Jewish Conscience*, 83.

LIST OF WORKS CITED

ECCLESIAL DOCUMENTS

Unless indicated otherwise, excerpts from the documents below have been sourced from the *Dialogika* online library maintained by the Council of Centers on Jewish-Christian Relations and the Institute for Jewish-Catholic Relations of Saint Joseph's University in Philadelphia, https://www.ccjr.us/dialogika-resources/documents-and-statements/roman-catholic.

Second Vatican Council

Dogmatic Constitution on the Church. *Lumen Gentium.* November 21, 1964.

Dogmatic Constitution on Divine Revelation. *Dei Verbum.* November 18, 1965.

Declaration on the Relationship of the Church to Non-Christian Religions. *Nostra Aetate.* October 28, 1965.

Declaration on Religious Freedom. *Dignitatis Humanae.* December 7, 1965.

Pope Pius XI

Reflection for Belgian pilgrims. Rome, September 6, 1938.

CATHOLIC-JEWISH RELATIONS

Pope Paul VI

Apostolic Exhortation. *Nobis in Animo.* March 25, 1974. https://www.vatican.va/content/paul-vi/it/apost_exhortations/documents/hf_p-vi_exh_19740325_nobis-in-animo.html.

Pope John Paul II

Address to Representatives of Jewish Organizations. Rome, March 12, 1979.

Address to Representatives of West German Jewish Community. Mainz, November 17, 1980.

Address to Episcopal Conference Delegates of the Pontifical Commission for Religious Relations with the Jews. March 6, 1982.

Address at the Great Synagogue of Rome. April 13, 1986.

Address to Jewish Community Leaders in Australia. November 26, 1986.

Address to the Pontifical Biblical Commission. April 11, 1997.

Address to a Vatican conference on "The Roots of Anti-Judaism in the Christian Milieu." October 31, 1997.

Letter, "Pilgrimage to Places Linked to the History of Salvation." June 29, 1999.

Homily at Mount Sinai. February 26, 2000.

Prayer at the Western Wall, Jerusalem. March 26, 2000.

Pope Benedict XVI

Address to American Jewish Delegation. Rome, February 12, 2009.

Greetings to the Chief Rabbis of Israel. May 12, 2009.

Post-Synodal Apostolic Exhortation on the Church in the Middle East. *Ecclesia in Medio Oriente.* September 14, 2012.

Post-Synodal Apostolic Exhortation on the Word of God in the Life and Mission of the Church. *Verbum Domini.* September 30, 2010.

List of Works Cited

The following titles are the personal writings of Joseph Ratzinger the theologian, not official documents of the papacy.

Joseph Ratzinger/Pope Benedict XVI. *Jesus of Nazareth. From the Baptism in the Jordan to the Transfiguration.* Translated by Adrian J. Walker. New York: Doubleday, 2007.

———. *Jesus of Nazareth, Part Two, Holy Week: From the Entrance into Jerusalem to the Resurrection.* San Francisco: Ignatius Press, 2011.

Emeritus Pope Benedict XVI. "Grace and Vocation without Remorse: Comments on the Treatise De Judaeis." *Communio International Review* 45 (July 2018): 163–84.

———. "Letter to Rabbi Arie Folger." August 23, 2018.

Pope Francis

Apostolic Exhortation on the Proclamation of the Gospel in Today's World. *Evangelii Gaudium.* November 24, 2013.

Papal visit to the Holy Land. Welcoming Address. May 26, 2014.

Address to the International Council of Christians and Jews. Rome, June 30, 2015.

Address at the Great Synagogue of Rome. January 17, 2016.

La Bibbia dell'Amicizia (The Bible of Friendship: Passages of the Torah/Pentateuch commented upon by Jews and Christians). Edited by Marco Cassuto Morselli and Giulio Michelin. MI, Italy: San Paolo Edizioni, 2019. Unofficial English translation of preface accessed at *Dialogika.* https://www.ccjr.us/dialogika-resources/documents-and-statements/roman-catholic/francis/francis-2018nov.

Vatican Commissions

Commission of the Holy See for Religious Relations with the Jews. "Guidelines and Suggestions for Implementing the Conciliar Declaration 'Nostra Aetate' (No. 4)." December 1, 1974.

———. "Notes on the Correct Way to Present the Jews and Judaism in Preaching and Catechesis in the Roman Catholic Church." June 24, 1985.

CATHOLIC-JEWISH RELATIONS

———. "We Remember: A Reflection on the Shoah." March 16, 1998.

———. "'The Gifts and the Calling of God Are Irrevocable' (Rom 11:29). A Reflection on Theological Questions Pertaining to Catholic-Jewish Relations on the Occasion of the 50th Anniversary of 'Nostra Aetate' (No. 4)." December 10, 2015.

International Theological Commission. "Memory and Reconciliation: The Church and the Faults of the Past." March 7, 1999.

Pontifical Biblical Commission. "The Jewish People and Their Sacred Scriptures in the Christian Bible." May 24, 2001.

Pontifical Council for Interreligious Dialogue. "Dialogue and Proclamation: Reflections and Orientations on Interreligious Dialogue and the Proclamation of the Gospel of Jesus Christ." May 19, 1991. https://www.vatican.va/roman_curia/pontifical_councils/interelg/documents/rc_pc_interelg_doc_19051991_dialogue-and-proclamatio_en.html.

Pontifical Council for the Promotion of New Evangelization. *Directory for Catechesis*. Libreria Editrice Vaticana, 2020. Australian edition: Homebush NSW: St Pauls Publications, 2020.

Catechism of the Catholic Church. Libreria Editrice Vaticana, 1993. https://www.vatican.va/archive/ENG0015/__PR.HTM.

Episcopal Conferences

Catholic Bishops of France. "Declaration of Repentance." September 30, 1997.

French Catholic Bishops' Committee for Relations with Jews. "Statement on Jewish-Christian Relations." April 16, 1973.

United States Conference of Catholic Bishops, Committee for Ecumenical and Interreligious Affairs. "Criteria for the Evaluation of Dramatizations of the Passion." Washington, DC: United States Conference of Catholic Bishops, 1988.

United States National Conference of Catholic Bishops. "Guidelines for Catholic-Jewish Relations." November 20, 1975.

List of Works Cited

Latin Patriarchate of Jerusalem

Latin Patriarch Pierbattista Pizzaballa. Reflection, "Jerusalem: Locus of the Soul." March 16, 2021. Latin Patriarchate of Jerusalem website. https://www.medialpj.org/latin-patriarch/jerusalem-locus-of-the-soul-a-mother-who-educates-and-makes-us-grow.html.

Jewish Statement

The Conference of European Rabbis, the Rabbinical Council of America, and the Chief Rabbinate of Israel. "Between Jerusalem and Rome: Reflections on 50 Years of *Nostra Aetate*." August 31, 2017.

Other Sources

Becker, Adam, and Yoshiko Reed, Annette., eds. *The Ways that Never Parted: Jews and Christians in Late Antiquity and the Early Middle Ages.* Minneapolis: Fortress, 2007.

Boys, Mary C., ed. *Seeing Judaism Anew: Christianity's Sacred Obligation.* Lanham, MD: Rowman & Littlefield, 2005.

Cassuto Morselli, Marco, and Giulio Michelin. *La Bibbia dell'Amicizia* (The Bible of Friendship: Passages of the Torah Pentateuch commented upon by Jews and Christians). Milan, Italy: San Paolo Edizioni, 2019. Unofficial English translation of preface by Pope Francis accessed at *Dialogika*, https://www.ccjr.us/dialogika-resources/documents-and-statements/roman-catholic/francis/francis-2018nov.

Cohen, Raymond. "Challenges of the Land and State of Israel for Christian Churches: The Example of the Vatican." In *Enabling Dialogue about the Land: A Resource Book for Christians and Jews,* edited by Philip A. Cunningham, Ruth Langer, and Jesper Svartvik, 191–212. Mahwah, NJ: Paulist Press, 2020.

Congar, Yves. *True and False Reform in the Church.* Rev. ed. Translated by Paul Philibert. Collegeville: Liturgical Press, 2011.

CATHOLIC-JEWISH RELATIONS

Connelly, John. *From Enemy to Brother: The Revolution in Catholic Teaching on the Jews 1933–1965.* Cambridge: Harvard University Press, 2012.

Cunningham, Philip A. *Education for Shalom: Religion Textbooks and the Enhancement of the Catholic and Jewish Relationship.* Collegeville, MN: Liturgical Press, 1995.

———. *Pondering the Passion: What's at Stake for Christians and Jews?* Lanham, MD: Rowman & Littlefield, 2004.

———. *Seeking Shalom: The Journey to Right Relationship between Catholics and Jews.* Grand Rapids, MI: Eerdmans, 2015.

———. "Toward a Catholic Theology of the Centrality of the Land." In *Enabling Dialogue about the Land: A Resource Book for Christians and Jews*, edited by Philip A. Cunningham, Ruth Langer, and Jesper Svartvik, 315–25. Mahwah, NJ: Paulist Press, 2020.

Dacy, Marianne. *The Separation of Early Christianity from Judaism.* New York: Cambria Press, 2010.

Dalin, David G., and Matthew Levering, eds. *John Paul II and the Jewish People: A Jewish-Christian Dialogue.* Lanham, MD: Rowman & Littlefield, 2008.

D'Costa, Gavin. *Catholic Doctrines on the Jewish People after Vatican II.* New York: Oxford University Press, 2019.

Donaldson, Terence L. *Jews and Anti-Judaism in the New Testament: Decision Points and Divergent Interpretations.* London: SPCK, 2010.

Fisher, Eugene J. "Official Roman Catholic Teaching on Jews and Judaism: Commentary and Context." In *In Our Time: The Flowering of Jewish-Catholic Dialogue*, edited by Eugene J. Fisher and Leon Klenicki, 3–18. Mahwah, NJ: Paulist Press, 1990.

Fredriksen, Paula. *When Christians Were Jews: The First Generation.* New Haven: Yale University Press, 2018.

Gregerman, Adam. "The Desirability of Jewish Conversion to Christianity in Contemporary Catholic Thought." *Horizons* 45, no. 2 (October 2018): 249–86.

List of Works Cited

———. "Is the Biblical Land Promise Irrevocable? Post-Nostra Aetate Catholic Theologies of the Jewish Covenant and the Land of Israel." *Modern Theology* 34 (April 2018): 137–58.

———. "Superiority without Supersessionism: Walter Kasper and The Gifts and the Calling of God are Irrevocable on the Status of God's Covenant with the Jews after Jesus." *Theological Studies* 79 (2018): 36–59.

Hammer, Reuven. *The Torah Revolution: Fourteen Truths that Changed the World*. Woodstock, VT: Jewish Lights, 2011.

Henrix, Hans Hermann. "The Son of God Became Human as a Jew: Implications of the Jewishness of Jesus for Christology." In *Christ Jesus and the Jewish People Today: New Explorations of Theological Interrelationships*, edited by Philip A. Cunningham, Joseph Sievers, Mary C. Boys, Hans Hermann Henrix, and Jesper Svartvik, 114–43. Grand Rapids, MI: Eerdmans, 2011.

Henze, Matthias. *Mind the Gap: How the Jewish Writings between the Old and New Testament Help Us Understand Jesus*. Minneapolis: Fortress, 2017.

Herzl, Theodore. *The Complete Diaries of Theodor Herzl*, translated by Harry Zohn. New York/London: Herzl Press, Thomas Yoseloff, 1960. Excerpt accessed at *Dialogika*. https://www.ccjr.us/dialogika-resources/primary-texts-from-the-history-of-the-relationship/herzl1904.

Heschel, Abraham Joshua. *Heavenly Torah as Refracted through the Generations*. Edited and translated by Gordon Tucker. New York: Continuum, 2007.

International Council of Christians and Jews. "A Time for Recommitment: Jewish-Christian Dialogue 70 Years after War and Shoah." https://www.iccj.org/fileadmin/ICCJ/pdf-Dateien/A_Time_for_Recommitment_engl.pdf.

Isaac, Jules. *The Teaching of Contempt. Christian Roots of Anti-Semitism*. Translated by Helen Weaver. 2nd ed. New York: McGraw-Hill, 1965.

Kader, Jamal. "Theology of the Land: A Christian Palestinian Perspective." In *Enabling Dialogue about the Land: A Resource Book for Christians and Jews*, edited by Philip A. Cunningham, Ruth

Langer, and Jesper Svartvik, 63–85. Mahwah, NJ: Paulist Press, 2020.

Kasper, Walter. Address to International Catholic-Jewish Liaison Committee re: the Declaration *Dominus Iesus*. New York, May 1, 2001. https://www.ccjr.us/dialogika-resources/documents-and-statements/roman-catholic/kasper/kasper01may1-1.

———. "Antisemitism: A Wound to Be Healed; Reflections for the Fourth European Day of Jewish Culture." September 5, 2003. https://www.ccjr.us/dialogika-resources/documents-and-statements/roman-catholic/kasper/wk03sept5.

———. "The Commission for Religious Relations with the Jews: A Crucial Endeavour of the Catholic Church." Address at Boston College. November 6, 2002. https://www.ccjr.us/dialogika-resources/documents-and-statements/roman-catholic/kasper/kasper02nov6-2.

Levenson, Jon. "Did God Forgive Adam? An Exercise in Comparative Midrash." In *Jews and Christians: People of God*, edited by Carl E. Braaten and Robert W. Jenson, 148–70. Grand Rapids, MI: Eerdmans, 2003.

———. *Inheriting Abraham: The Legacy of the Patriarch in Judaism, Christianity and Islam*. Princeton, NJ: Princeton University Press, 2012.

Levine, Amy-Jill. *The Misunderstood Jew: The Church and the Scandal of the Jewish Jesus*. San Francisco: Harper Collins, 2006.

Levine, Amy-Jill, and Marc Zvi Brettler, eds. *The Bible with and without Jesus: How Jews and Christians Read the Same Stories Differently*. New York: HarperCollins, 2020.

———. *The Jewish Annotated New Testament*. 2nd ed. New York: Oxford University Press, 2017.

Lubac, Henri de. *The Motherhood of the Church*. Translated by Sergia Englund. San Francisco: Ignatius Press, 1982.

Lux, Richard. *The Jewish People, the Holy Land, and the State of Israel: A Catholic View*. Mahwah, NJ: Paulist Press, 2010.

Madigan, Kevin J., and Jon D. Levenson. *Resurrection: The Power of God for Christians and Jews*. New Haven: Yale University Press, 2008.

List of Works Cited

Marshall, Bruce D. "Religion and Election: Aquinas on Natural Law, Judaism, and Salvation in Christ." *Nova et Vetera* 14, no. 1 (2016): 61–125.

O'Collins, Gerald. *Inspiration: Towards a Christian Interpretation of Biblical Inspiration.* New York: Oxford University Press, 2018.

O'Shea, Paul. *A Cross Too Heavy: Pope Pius XII and the Jews of Europe.* New York: Macmillan, 2011.

Pawlikowski, John T. *Restating the Catholic Church's Relationship with the Jewish People: The Challenge of Super-Sessionary Theology.* New York: Edwin Mellen, 2013.

———. "Toward A Theology of Belonging: A Catholic Christian Perspective." In *Enabling Dialogue about the Land: A Resource Book for Christians and Jews*, edited by Philip A. Cunningham, Ruth Langer, and Jesper Svartvik, 262–81. Mahwah, NJ: Paulist Press, 2020.

———. "The Uniqueness of the Christian-Jewish Dialogue: A Yes and a No." *Studies in Christian-Jewish Relations* 12 (2017): 1–14. https://doi.org/10.6017/scjr.v12i1.9799.

Sacks, Jonathan. *Leviticus: The Book of Holiness; Covenant & Conversation*, vol. 3. Jerusalem: Koren Publishers, 2015. Kindle Edition.

———. "The Way of Responsibility: The Jewish Future." *Ten Paths to God.* Unit 10. https://www.rabbisacks.org/curriculum-resources/ten-paths-to-god/.

Salmon, Marilyn J. *Preaching without Contempt: Overcoming Unintended Anti-Judaism.* Minneapolis: Augsburg Fortress, 2006.

Soloveitchik, Joseph B. "Confrontation." In *Bridges. Documents of the Christian-Jewish Dialogue*, vol. 1, edited by Franklin Sherman, 405–18. New York: Paulist Press, 2011.

Tapie, Matthew A. *Aquinas on Israel and the Church: The Question of Supersessionism in the Theology of Thomas Aquinas.* Eugene, OR: Pickwick, 2014.

Tobias, Norman. *Jewish Conscience of the Church: Jules Isaac and the Second Vatican Council.* Cham, Switzerland: Springer International, 2017.

CATHOLIC-JEWISH RELATIONS

Trainor, Michael. "Understanding Land and Its Ecological Connectedness: Implications for Christian-Jewish Dialogue." In *Enabling Dialogue about the Land: A Resource Book for Christians and Jews*, edited by Philip A. Cunningham, Ruth Langer, and Jesper Svartvik, 335–54. Mahwah, NJ: Paulist Press, 2020.

Zetterholm, Magnus. *Approaches to Paul: A Student's Guide to Recent Scholarship*. Minneapolis: Fortress, 2009.

Websites Cited

Dialogika: the website for Council of Centers on Christian-Jewish Dialogue. www.ccjr.us/dialogika-resources

Institute for Jewish-Catholic Relations, Saint Joseph's University, Philadelphia. www.sju.edu/college-arts-and-sciences/ijcr/

International Holocaust Remembrance Alliance (IHRA) website. www.holocaustremembrance.com

Shalom Hartman Institute, Jerusalem (Jewish research and education institute). www.hartman.org.il

Saint James Vicariate for Hebrew-Speaking Catholics in Israel. www.catholic.co.il

Vatican website: www.vatican.va

Further links of interest

Bat Kol International (Christians learning from Judaism). www.batkolinternational.com

Cardinal Bea Centre for Judaic Studies. www.unigre.it/en/judaic-studies

Etz-Hayim—Tree of Life Publishing (Christians learning from Judaism). www.etz-hayim.com

International Council of Christians & Jews. www.iccj.org

ISPS-Ratisbonne. Bat Kol-Christian Centre for Jewish Studies. www.ratisbonne.org.il

Light of Torah.net (Christians learning from Judaism). www.lightoftorah.net

The Notre Dame de Sion Centre for Biblical Formation, Jerusalem. www.biblicalformationcentre.com

OTHER VOLUMES IN THIS SERIES

Clemens Thoma and Michael Wyschogrod, eds., *Understanding Scripture: Explorations of Jewish and Christian Traditions of Interpretation* (1987; e-book only)

Bernard J. Lee, *The Galilean Jewishness of Jesus: Retrieving the Origins of Christianity (Conversation on the Road Not Taken, Vol. I)* (1988; e-book only)

Clemens Thoma and Michael Wyschogrod, eds., *Parable and Story in Judaism and Christianity* (1989)

Eugene J. Fisher, ed., *Interwoven Destinies: Jews and Christians through the Ages* (1992; e-book only)

George M. Smiga, *Pain and Polemic: Anti-Judaism in the Gospels* (1992; e-book only)

Anthony J. Kenny, *Catholics, Jews, and the State of Israel* (1993; e-book only)

Eugene J. Fisher, ed., *Visions of the Other: Jewish and Christian Theologians Assess the Dialogue* (1994; e-book only)

Vincent Martin, *A House Divided: The Parting of the Ways between Synagogue and Church* (1995; e-book only)

Leon Klenicki and Geoffrey Wigoder, *A Dictionary of the Jewish-Christian Dialogue* (1995; e-book only)

Frank E. Eakin Jr., *What Price Prejudice? Christian Antisemitism in America* (1998)

Philip A. Cunningham and Arthur F. Starr, eds., *Sharing Shalom: A Process for Local Interfaith Dialogue between Christians and Jews* (1999)

Ekkehard Schuster and Reinhold Boschert-Kimmig, *Hope against Hope: Johann Baptist Metz and Elie Wiesel Speak Out on the Holocaust* (1999)

Mary C. Boys, *Has God Only One Blessing? Judaism as a Source of Christian Self-Understanding* (2000)

Johannes Reuchlin, translated and edited by Peter Wortsman, *Recommendation Whether to Confiscate, Destroy and Burn All Jewish Books: A Classic Treatise against Anti-Semitism* (2000)

Avery Dulles and Leon Klenicki, *The Holocaust, Never to Be Forgotten: Reflections on the Holy See's Document* We Remember (2001)

Philip A. Cunningham, *A Story of Shalom: The Calling of Christians and Jews by a Covenanting God* (2001; e-book only)

Philip A. Cunningham, *Sharing the Scriptures: The Word Set Free, Volume 1* (2003)

Dina Wardi, *Auschwitz: Contemporary Jewish and Christian Encounters* (2003)

Michael Lotker, *A Christian's Guide to Judaism* (2004)

Edward H. Flannery, *The Anguish of the Jews: Twenty-Three Centuries of Antisemitism* (Revised and Updated) (2004)

Lawrence Boadt, CSP, and Kevin di Camillo, eds., *John Paul II in the Holy Land: In His Own Words; With Christian and Jewish Perspectives by Yehezkel Landau and Michael McGarry, CSP* (2005)

James K. Aitken and Edward Kessler, eds., *Challenges in Jewish-Christian Relations* (2006)

Steven C. Boguslawski, OP, *Thomas Aquinas on the Jews: Insights into His Commentary on Romans 9–11* (2008)

George M. Smiga, *The Gospel of John Set Free: Preaching without Anti-Judaism* (2008)

Daniel J. Harrington, SJ, *The Synoptic Gospels Set Free: Preaching without Anti-Judaism* (2009)

Richard C. Lux, *The Jewish People, the Holy Land, and the State of Israel: A Catholic View* (2009)

Cardinal Jean-Marie Lustiger, edited by Jean Duchesne, *Cardinal Jean-Marie Lustiger on Christians and Jews* (2010)

Pope Benedict XVI, *Pope Benedict XVI in the Holy Land* (2010)

Thomas G. Casey and Justin Taylor, eds., *Paul's Jewish Matrix* (2011)

Franklin Sherman, ed., *Bridges—Documents of the Christian-Jewish Dialogue: Volume One—The Road to Reconciliation (1945–1985)* (2011)

Eugene J. Fisher, eds., Memoria Futuri: *Catholic-Jewish Dialogue Yesterday, Today, and Tomorrow; Texts and Addresses of Cardinal William H. Keeler* (2012)

Mary C. Boys, *Redeeming Our Sacred Story: The Death of Jesus and Relations between Jews and Christians* (2013)

Celia M. Deutsch, Eugene J. Fisher, and James Rudin, eds., *Toward the Future: Essays on Catholic-Jewish Relations in Memory of Rabbi León Klenicki* (2013)

Franklin Sherman, ed., *Bridges—Documents of the Christian-Jewish Dialogue: Volume Two—Building a New Relationship (1986–2013)* (2014)

Ronald Kronish, ed., *Coexistence and Reconciliation in Israel: Voices for Interreligious Dialogue* (2015)

Elena G. Procario-Foley and Robert A. Cathey, eds., *Righting Relations after the Holocaust and Vatican II: Essays in Honor of John Pawlikowski, OSM* (2018)

Paula Fredriksen and Jesper Svartvik, eds., *Krister among the Jews and Gentiles* (2018)

Carol Rittner, Stephen D. Smith, and Irena Steinfeldt. *The Holocaust and the Christian World: Reflections on the Past, Challenges for the Future*, 2nd edition (2019)

STIMULUS BOOKS are developed by the Stimulus Foundation, a not-for-profit organization, and are published by Paulist Press. The Foundation wishes to further the publication of scholarly books on Jewish and Christian topics that are of importance to Judaism and Christianity.

The Stimulus Foundation was established by an erstwhile refugee from Nazi Germany who intends to contribute with these publications to the improvement of communication between Jews and Christians.

Books for publication in this series will be selected by a committee of the Foundation, and offers of manuscripts and works in progress should be addressed to:

The Stimulus Foundation
c/o Paulist Press
997 Macarthur Boulevard
Mahwah, NJ 07430
www.paulistpress.com

www.ingramcontent.com/pod-product-compliance
Lightning Source LLC
Chambersburg PA
CBHW071841230426
43671CB00012B/2025